NEWS FROM THE TOPE

DAVE ERMINI

ISBN: 1480046922
ISBN-13: 978-1480046924

To Nancy

CONTENTS

DAVE ERMINI

THE CONVERSATION

I wasn't sure at first if I wanted to tell them about The Tope. While it wasn't a state secret by any means, we had always been wary of bringing any attention to ourselves, at least until The Tope had been firmly established and was ready to expand. As the conversation progressed, however, it became clear to me that I was going to have to tell them everything and quite possibly show them the place itself, for they would never understand and certainly never believe me if I did not. The Tope was nearly ready to move into its next phase of development, after all. And wasn't enlightenment what it had been all about in the first place? In any case, our ability to persuade outsiders would be vital in our future expansion efforts. And so it was that I decided to spill my guts.

As our twenty-year high school reunion approached, a core group of my classmates had decided to meet up with one another near our alma mater, Barr Academy, an exclusive private preparatory school in the heart of the City. Apart from these school reunions, we rarely saw one another. Some of us had moved out of the city, even though we all worked here, and the various commutes, coupled with our busy schedules prevented us from meeting more often. At reunion times though, we talked and laughed and argued as though we had never been apart. As we had done on our previous reunions, we decided to meet at our favorite juvenile watering hole, Paradisio Perduto, a local tavern notorious for its cheap drinks and abundant food. This being a Saturday afternoon, it was also reasonably quiet; a good atmosphere for the debate that was the inevitable result of our gathering. Mike, Frank, and I had all played football, basketball, and baseball together on our school teams. Frank and I, both from working-class families, had received full athletic scholarships. Mike and Alex, however, came from the other side of the tracks. Mike was the son of a nationally renowned neurosurgeon; and Alex, now married to Mike, was a tomboy/intellectual who had hung out during our school days, with our mixed crowd of brains and jocks. She was the daughter of a hedge fund manager – one of the wealthiest men in the country - but we never held that against her. After graduating, Mike had become an attorney, Frank had gone into the family trucking business, Alex was a tenured social anthropologist at the University, and I chose a profession that would forever doom me to a life of relative poverty. I became an Architect.

Since the tavern was located on the fringes of a rundown part of town, the talk always turned to how bad things had become in the City since we had used the area as our stomping grounds. And today was no different.

Mike: Wow! This place sure has changed since we were in school here! I can remember walking through this neighborhood at all hours of the day and night back then. Today I was nervous just walking across the street from the parking garage. How did it happen?

Alex: Technology, actually. Cities like this one that were founded on commerce and manufacturing, suffered when improved transportation systems allowed both people and industries to move out to the suburbs and more recently to relocate overseas. And with telecommuting, the Internet, and the information age upon us, it promises to get even worse. New technologies have allowed the white collar managerial class - people like us - to conveniently relocate to the suburbs while still working in the City. We make our money here, use all of the best city services, and then live and pay taxes in small suburban towns.

But because blue collar manufacturing jobs are becoming scarcer and scarcer, those who are unable to obtain employment in these higher wage managerial and service positions are caught between a rock and a hard place. And the drain of taxable income from the City to the suburbs leaves a mass of people behind. The end result has been that those who are most in need of help receive the least.

Frank: Least my ass! We've been paying out millions of dollars to the so-called "less fortunate" for decades, and look at the good it's done! And let me tell you something, Alex, these people aren't "unfortunate." They're not unlucky. They're friggin' lazy! In this country, if you want to make something of your life, all you have to do is work for it. Just look at me and Dave here. We weren't born to wealth like you two. We made it the old fashioned way. We worked our butts off!

You know, we tried to reduce the hand-out mentality in this country a few years back with that Welfare to Work legislation, but the politicians somehow keep coming up with new ways to perpetuate it. Now families that pay absolutely squat in taxes, get an "earned income" tax credit, which in my mind is nothing more than a wealth redistribution scheme. I thought we fought and won the Cold War to put an end to Socialist ideas like that. But no. Here they come again - only this time within our own country!

I live in the suburbs too Alex, but I'll guarantee you that I'm paying a hell of a lot more in taxes than I get back in governmental services. When you add it all up, I'll bet the government takes half or more of what I earn, if you consider social security, state, federal, sales taxes, gasoline taxes, liquor and tobacco taxes, tolls, and so forth. Most people don't even realize how much they're actually paying in taxes, because it gets spread out over so many things. But to me, it doesn't matter whether they take it from my paycheck or when I'm filling up my gas tank. Once they take it, it's not in my wallet.

And do you know where it all goes? To feed an over-bloated Federal bureaucracy, foreign aid to countries that hate us, and to pay for the two wars that serve only to support the military industrial complex Eisenhower warned us about years ago. But mostly, it goes to all of these "unfortunate" people and corporate special interests all feeding like pigs at the public trough. And the worst thing about it is that instead of gratitude for the money we provide them with, we get nothing but hatred and resentment in return for our gift. I left the City to get away from people like that.

Dave: But here's the problem Frank. When good, hard-working people leave cities rather than help to battle the urban problems that they are fleeing, it forces cities into a downward spiral of decay, as Alex says. And that's exactly what has occurred in virtually every big city in America over the last few decades. We need to find ways to encourage the managerial class, people like ourselves, to move back into the cities, because we need all of the resources that they bring with them - financial, intellectual, and political.

Now I'm not saying that we should in any way **force** people to live in the city, I'm saying that if cities don't find novel ways to attract people back in, then they are doomed to a slow death that will cost **everybody** in the long run.

Mike: Well I agree with you in principal, Dave, but there are too many problems in the cities - drugs, crime, gang violence, poverty, pollution, bad schools, the homeless. All of these things tend to drive people away from the City - especially those who have young children or those who want to start a family. Who in their right mind wants their kid growing up next to a slum?

Alex: There have been slums or ghettos or the equivalent as long as there have been cities, Mike. There have always been costs associated with living in densely populated areas. That's the trade-off of living a metropolitan lifestyle. It just seems that lately, even though crime rates are supposedly down, that urban pathologies are affecting younger and younger children. You hear all the time now about six and seven year old kids involved in gang violence or drugs. That's what is really shocking to me. And I don't know what we can do to stop it.

Frank: You know, I thought that ending "welfare as we know it" was going to turn this city around, but it hasn't. It's still just as filthy and unsafe. Dealers are still selling drugs on every street corner. The panhandlers and winos are still harassing people. And hookers are still strolling the streets. But it wasn't always that way. This city used to be a hell of a lot safer! I remember my parents telling me how they used to sleep on the fire escape at night when it got too hot in their apartment during the summer. And my grandparents used to take blankets over to The Park and sleep on the ground. Anyone who would even consider doing that today needs to get their head examined. They'd probably never make it to the park in the first place - they'd be mugged or raped or both before they even got there!

Mike: Until this latest financial meltdown, I actually think that it had gotten a little better. People were starting to have hope that they could own their own home and make lives for themselves and their kids a little bit better. But then everyone – the mortgage lenders, the regulators, the investors, the politicians, as well as all those people with multiple mortgages flipping houses - got a little too greedy, and nobody at the top was willing to put the brakes on. And before anyone realized it we were all flying off the cliff. But it will turn around again. It always does.

It's going to take a little time to take hold. When the economy starts picking up again, people will start to realize that they are personally responsible for earning their keep. It will be a long hard slog, but I really believe that eventually we will be better off. People may not be able to get the types of jobs that they had in the past but the work will eventually come and there is dignity in providing for yourself and your family. There is no dignity and certainly no pride that comes from picking up a welfare check or an unemployment check every month.

Alex: Yes, but I saw some of the jobs that were created for those who were forced off of welfare. And I fear that the same thing will occur in the future. There's not that much dignity in sweeping dog crap off of a street corner or breaking your back in a sweatshop for minimum wage.

Frank: Sorry Alex, but I don't buy that! There is nothing wrong with putting in a hard day's work no matter what the work is.

There was a time in this country when people would do just about anything to avoid having to take a handout. My grandfather worked most of his life making minimum wage, and he did some of the most disgusting, back-breaking labor you could think of. When he could, he worked two or three jobs - whatever it took to provide for his family. And there were probably some lean, desperate years back in the Depression days. A lot worse than what we are going through now. Back then if you didn't find a way to provide for yourself, you didn't eat. But I think he would have rather starved to death than take something that he didn't earn with his own labor. He busted his ass for years and he never thought once about himself. All he wanted was to make life for his kids a little bit better than his own. And he did.

It was called The American Dream. I wonder what's happened to it....

Mike: Well, up until the financial collapse, it was alive and well Frank. You're just not looking for it in the right place. Immigration patterns have changed, man. We're not adding Irish, Italians, or Germans to our population anymore. Look at all the Asians, Eastern Europeans and Middle Easterners coming in - even the illegals from Mexico and Central America that we like to complain about so much. African Americans and Latinos were becoming more affluent. They were all doing exactly the same thing that your grandfather did, and they were assimilating into the American economy and culture just like the Europeans did decades ago - at a slower pace, I'll grant you - but assimilating just the same.

The problem that I see now, especially with all of these "Occupy" groups – although I am sympathetic to those who are out of work, who are upset that those who created the problem seem to have made out the best, and who simply want to have a decent job - is that a culture of permanent dependency has developed in this country among some of us, and it is going to be awfully difficult to break that mindset - the belief that it is the responsibility of others to take care of me if things don't work out exactly as I would like.

People are living their entire lives with the expectation that the Federal government will provide all of their food, housing and clothing, and will now provide them with free health care. When you start with that kind of outlook on life, and all of your political and spiritual leaders are telling you that you are the victim, that you can never get ahead because of crony capitalism, racism, and nepotism, and you then add problems like gang violence, teenage pregnancy, and substance abuse into the mix, you almost doom a class of people to failure. And by the way it has nothing to do with race – although Blacks and Hispanics are certainly disproportionately affected – it is about culture. It is about what we, as Americans, want the role of our government to be.

Alex: Well if we really want to help people get out of these cycles of dependency we are going to have to spend some money. What we really need to do is invest in people - provide them with vocational training so that they can find better jobs. Single mothers will need free day care so that they can lead productive lives. And those with drug and alcohol addiction problems need treatment, not jail time. We need to find places to care for all the homeless. And for God sake, we need to ban handguns. I don't want to hear another news story about some teenage kid going on a shooting spree in his school! It's got to end!

Frank: What we really need is more jails, more beat cops on the street, and more arrests of people who are committing crimes. We need "broken window" policies to be used by law enforcement so that crime doesn't escalate out of control. When it comes to guns, we would do just fine if we only enforced all of the gun laws that we have already. Don't try to take them away from the law-abiding citizens who are just trying to protect themselves! And as for the so-called homeless, we should take all of these bums off of the street and force them to either live in shelters or go to mental hospitals or get a job like the rest of us.

Free day care, Alex? What are you insane? I have enough trouble paying for my own kid's day care without having to pay for somebody else's children. Why is it that whenever liberals talk about fixing the ills of society, it always involves taking money out of my pocket and giving it to someone else?

Alex: Why is it that conservatives always want to turn America into some sort of fascist police state? Don't you have any compassion within you? There are people living in the inner city that need help. We are still the wealthiest nation on the face of the Earth. We should be able to take care of our most needy.

Frank: Hey, I'm all for taking care of people who truly need a hand to help them out of a tight spot. I just don't want people abusing the system at my expense. It used to be that charities and churches did most of the work of helping out the needy with direct contributions from the people who lived in the community. They did a pretty good job of it too.

But then the federal government had to get involved. It all got started with the best of intentions. Nobody could argue with what they were trying to accomplish. But before long, a lot of people started to think that collecting a check from Uncle Sam was sort of their job. I see the same thing starting to happen with these extensions of unemployment benefits and all the new social welfare programs the leftist politicians want to ram down our throats.

All I'm saying is that you don't always have to spend money to help people out. Sometimes people need a kick in the ass more than they need a hug.

Alex: Sometimes people who get lost in the woods need help finding their way out. And if they are hungry, tired, and beaten they are going to need food, shelter and medical attention before they can get any better. All of that takes money.

Mike: I don't object to spending money, Alex, but I don't want us to give it away senselessly either. The big problem that I have with all of you bleeding hearts is that you often want to do anything that will make YOU feel better - absolve YOU of whatever guilt you may have - and not necessarily solve the problem at hand. I don't know how many times over the last two decades I've heard people on the left say "Well we have to do SOMETHING!"

You know what, doing nothing is sometimes better than doing something, if doing something means flushing money down the toilet.

Alex: How profound!

Mike: Oh, up yours!

Frank: Settle down class! Hey Dave you've been awfully quiet over there. You're supposed to be the problem solver, aren't you? What do you think we need to do to get this country back on track?

Dave: Well, I agree with Alex that money will need to be invested in our cities and that we, as a people, are capable and morally obligated to do so. There is an old saying that goes "For America to be Great, she must first be Good." And I agree with that. We have to take care of those who are truly in need and provide all those who are capable – regardless of race, gender, or ethnicity - with the opportunity to advance themselves. But I also agree with Mike that we need to invest this money sensibly, and that means having a coherent and long range plan that both liberals and conservatives, Republicans and Democrats can agree upon and are willing to implement together.

Mike: It can't be done.

Dave: Oh sure it can. But the solution will not involve simple one-shot fixes. That's the approach that has always failed us in the past. A lot of people in this country think that we have an economic crisis, a drug crisis, an educational crisis, a values crisis, or that racial relations is the root of all our problems. Well it is all of those things and none of those things at the same time. Urban decay is a process, not a singular problem fixed in time. To defeat it we are going to have to counter it with an opposing process pushing steadily against it.

Personally, I believe that most people in life follow the path of least resistance. If a person has been raised to respect the rule of law and the rights of others, to value hard work, and has been guided by caring parents and family, and has encountered negative consequences whenever he has strayed from what is good, then the path of least resistance for that person will be to lead a life that is ethical, industrious, loving, and just. Doing anything otherwise creates moral conflicts within that person that are simply unbearable.

Too often in our inner cities, however, children are raised with little guidance, in environments that seem devoid of any hope. The only role models they see are people who are engaged in lawless and immoral behaviors that go unchecked and without immediate punishment. Often, it is not because that child's parent or parents isn't trying to do the right thing. It's just that there are too many negative influences, beyond their control, pushing that child in the wrong direction. And some adults have already succumbed to these influences themselves and offer no help to their children at all. For these children, the path of least resistance is a path leading into a downward spiral of crime, addiction and ignorance.

Of course there are exceptions to this rule. There are plenty of examples of individuals who grew up in the most deplorable conditions, who managed to lift themselves up, somehow, by their own bootstraps. Likewise, there are many instances of individuals who were raised in supportive environments who turned into deviants or psychopaths. But in general, I think that the path of least resistance theory holds true. And so I think that for any process to work in our inner cities, it must remove all obstacles that would otherwise push people down the wrong path, and create tangible incentives for people to move up the correct one.

The solution will not work overnight. And it will not work equally effectively for everyone. But if it works for a majority of the people, in varying degrees, then it will be enough. A number of things need to be done - and all at the same time. We need to ensure that there are opportunities for all of those who are capable and who have the desire to succeed. And these opportunities must be legitimate, tangible, and realistic to everyone in the community. We also have to get the entire community involved in the success of every individual, but make it self-evident that the individual is solely responsible for his or her success or failure. We have to somehow minimize all of the negative influences that bombard people living in the inner cities, and we have to provide punishments for even the slightest of transgressions, but in a way that is equitable and just, and ultimately beneficial both to the transgressor and the community as a whole.

We have to find ways to provide quality education to the children and job training and career building opportunities to their parents. And lastly, we have to give good, law-abiding people the ability to maintain their own safety and health.

Alex: Well that sounds great, Dave, but how do you make all that happen?

Dave: What would you say if I told you that I know of a place right here in this city, where people are doing exactly what I'm talking about?

Frank: I'd say, what have you been smoking? 'Cause I want some!

Dave: I'm serious!

Alex: O.K. I'll bite! Where is this place, Dave?

Dave: It's a twenty-five square block section of the City near King Street. I moved there three years ago.

Frank: Are you out of your mind?!? That's got to be one of the worst areas of the city!

Alex: No offense Dave, but I'm with Frank on this one. If it's the place I'm thinking about, it looks like a war zone - nothing but burned up old buildings, drug dealers, gangs and addicts.

Dave: Yes it is the place you're thinking about. And no, it does not look like a war zone. At least, not anymore!

And so it was that I decided to tell them the story of "The Tope", as we came to call it; how it was formed, and how those of us who colonized it managed to turn one of the bleakest areas of the City into an island of hope amidst a sea of despair.

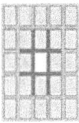

ORIGINS

It has always struck me as being somewhat ironic that within walking distance of some of the most expensive real estate on the planet, sits one of the world's most dangerous and forbidding slums. The Tope was an effort to try and do something about that. It was also an attempt to create a model inner city community that could be replicated throughout the country. How did we do it? Quite simply, actually - we bought ourselves a city. Well not a city really, but a good enough chunk of it to establish critical mass so that a core area could start to flourish and expand outward. You see, once you own something, you have the freedom to manipulate it as you see fit - you have control over it. So the first phase of The Tope was the acquisition of the property.

Now I know what you are asking yourselves right now. How did it ever get started in the first place, how did I get involved with it, and how come you haven't heard of it until now? I will answer those and other questions in good time, my friends, but to do that, I must first tell you about a small book that I wrote, years ago. This book, which is largely unknown and has never been published, was a description of a mythical neighborhood located within an unidentified inner city slum. It attempted to point out, whimsically and satirically, the problems that are causing contemporary cities to decay. It described a place where these problems had been confronted through a variety of innovative programs and institutions.

Although unknown to the general public at large, it has nevertheless been the catalyst behind the revitalization of this small community. You will see why this was so as I explain the events that transpired. What was the book? That's hard to explain actually, unless you were to read it, but it was, in essence, a modern day adaptation of Thomas More's *Utopia*.

Let me explain....

I started writing the book, as I said, years ago, but it really began when I was still a graduate architectural student at The University. During my final year there I participated in what was probably the most unusual design studio course ever given in an architectural school. This course focused on the notion of utopia, and what the term has meant to architects throughout history. The students were asked to compile a bibliography of any literature published throughout the ages that dealt with utopian thought and were then asked to read and report their findings back to the rest of the class.

A substantial amount of time was devoted to analyzing Thomas More's *Utopia* from both a literary and architectural perspective; the latter involved developing analytical diagrams and visual images of the mythical city described by More. The last half of the semester was a free-for-all; students were allowed to pursue a plan of study of their own choosing. Since this was an architectural school, mostly this meant coming up with one's own utopian vision and presenting city plans, and perspective renderings in the final review (or "jury" as it is called in architectural schools).

I took a different approach. After reading through *Utopia*, it became apparent to me that More wasn't describing some mythical faraway place as he suggests in the first part of his book, and wasn't merely satirizing his own country and city, but was in fact describing a tongue-in-cheek transformation of his actual city - London of 1516. And after analyzing the book from an architectural perspective, I realized that the geography, the buildings and infrastructure that were described in More's book bore a striking resemblance to the actual geography, buildings and infrastructure of London and England of that time. After

14

coming to this realization it all made sense to me, and I knew what I had to do. I decided to investigate in greater depth the extent to which passages of More's book related directly to specific structures, customs, or political situations in More's actual city. And since many of the allusions that More was making are lost upon modern ears, a great deal of research was required to document my thesis. After scouring the University libraries for any historical accounts and visual representation of 16th century London that I could get my hands on, I was ready to proceed with the next logical step.

At the final jury, I presented several boards that provided a visual and verbal comparison of the two cities, London of 1516 vs. More's Aircastle (the capital city of the island called Utopia). Each board had an image of 16th Century London adjacent to a similar image showing the same scene as transformed into Aircastle; below each image was a description of the scene, one taken out of a history text and the other out of More's book.

After my presentation was complete, the jurors commented. They seemed to have mixed emotions as to the worth of my study. One professor thought it was brilliant. Another complained that although my visual comparison was well and good, there was a set of drawings that was missing. "I don't see any Dave here!" he said. "Where is Dave's Utopia?"

The point he was making of course was that regardless of the success of my research, what was really important in an architectural school was how this knowledge was then applied in the design process to produce one's own work. And his suggestion was that I should have produced a third set of drawings, which depicted the city as I would have transformed it; my own utopian vision of 16th Century London.

He was right, of course, and the criticism stung for quite some time. But although this was valid criticism, what disturbed me about it was that London of 1516, or even London of 1987 for that matter, was not my city. It didn't belong to me.

Now let me say right here that there is an unspoken precept amongst many architectural academicians - one that I don't happen to subscribe to - that all the ills of society could be solved if only a talented architect (preferably oneself) were allowed to redesign the urban "fabric" - as though the structures are completely unrelated to the people who build them and inhabit them. It is the belief that one can change people by changing their surroundings.

I, on the other hand, have always believed that the opposite is true; that it is the culture of the time and place that is channeled by a competent architect into the built form; that architects and designers have the responsibility only to create beauty and order out of the chaos, one building or work of art at a time. And I certainly do not believe that any urban master plan, no matter how well thought out and beautifully designed, can, by itself, mold individuals into a desired societal ideal.

Rather, I believe that the best master plans are the reflection – filtered through the imaginative mind of the designer - of the prevailing urban thinking and market forces of the time. And if you are interested in transforming a city, you have to start, as More did, by transforming the people themselves: their customs, their political structure, their institutions, etc. And that as the people and their culture change, the urban fabric and the individual structures will inevitably reflect this change.

But I digress.

Upon graduating from the University, I decided to move back to the City to begin my career as an architect. I found a job with a small firm that specialized in, among other things, the restoration and rehabilitation of tenement housing. Part of my job involved surveying and documenting the existing condition of abandoned buildings slated for rehab which were located in neglected areas of the City. The job did not pay exceedingly well, and since I was not independently wealthy, and did not wish to have roommates, I faced the option of either living in the suburbs and commuting into work each day by train, or living in a slum within the city.

It angered me somewhat that I could not live the urban lifestyle that I was looking for without putting my life in danger. All that being said, in the end, I grudgingly chose the suburbs. Each day, on my way to and from work I would sit in my hermetically sealed train car and pass through the urban wasteland on the fringes of town. After so many years in the bucolic serenity of a college town, it was shocking to realize that many people in the heart of the City still lived in such deplorable conditions.

You see, I had traveled through these areas many times during my youth. My father, a detective in the City Police force, had been stationed in one of the most crime-ridden areas of the City. He was also involved in a local athletic league for children, of which my brother and I were members, and he often arranged sporting events and tournaments in the area, as well as fundraisers for the Police Athletic League. My mother had been an English teacher in a public elementary school located in one of the poorest sections of the City. And so for a variety of reasons, a lot of my youth was spent in and around "the slums", although my family lived in a more respectable blue-collar neighborhood elsewhere in the City.

Both of my parents used to lament about the conditions that the people in these areas were living in. And both of them experienced first hand the disruption that was caused to a majority of decent people by a minority of lawless, unprincipled individuals.

It was therefore quite depressing for me to discover that some twenty years later, life in the inner city hadn't gotten any better. In fact, it had gotten decidedly worse. And so it was, while sitting on the train one day, passing through the still blighted slums of my youth and recollecting my college professor's stinging criticism, that I had my epiphany.

Wouldn't it be interesting, I thought, to write a new version of *Utopia* that was a satire of our modern City? It could point out all of the problems of our modern slums and propose a solution, in the form of an idealized neighborhood. It could be written in such a way that the unsuspecting might believe that I was describing a real place, and that this neighborhood had actually been built. In the end, people might begin to realize that such a place was not a pipe dream at all, but was in fact, perfectly feasible.

And so I set about writing *Dave's Utopia*. Not being a professional writer or especially adept at the art, it took me several years of off and on writing to complete. After finally finishing the book, I researched the publishing industry in an effort to get the book published. For unsolicited works, such as this, most publishers did not want to read an entire manuscript - only a synopsis of the work and a couple sample chapters. I prepared scores of submittal packages outlining the book, and even wrote down some ideas in my cover letters on how I thought the book could be marketed. I excitedly sent out these packages, keen with anticipation, awaiting the day when I would make myself and my idealized City known to the public.

I waited for weeks on end for the replies, certain that I was soon to become a celebrity. But my enthusiasm turned quickly to disappointment as the rejection notices poured into my mailbox, informing me that my manuscript and I were not ready for prime time. I was completely devastated when the final rejection letter arrived in my mailbox, and I fell into a deep depression that lasted for several weeks. But then one day, many months later, I received a letter from Douglas Brothers Incorporated, expressing an interest in my book. The letter was excruciatingly brief, requesting only that I meet with them on the following Monday to discuss my manuscript.

What was really strange about this, though, was that I had not a submitted a package to any entity named Douglas Brothers, Inc., and in fact had never even heard of the company prior to receiving the letter. I would soon find out why.

The Brothers

The return address on the letter I received indicated that Douglas Brothers, Inc. was located uptown, in a more industrial part of the City. And when I looked them up, I discovered that they were not a publishing house at all. I found, to my astonishment, that Douglas Brothers, Inc. made bread.

O.K. not just bread. Actually, as I was soon to find out, they were a gigantic commercial bakery that produced a whole range of baked goods and distributed them throughout the region under various brand names. But what the hell did they want from me then, I wondered?

Then again, I thought, what did I have to lose? Absolutely nothing!

And so, the following Monday, I took the day off from work, traveled uptown, and arrived at the specified address. There, I found a massive, nondescript, brick factory building bearing the Douglas Brothers, Incorporated banner in paint that had worn off decades ago. I located the entrance and walked into the reception area where I was greeted pleasantly and asked to wait in a small conference room, where I was told, The Brothers would meet me momentarily. After a few minutes had gone by, three gentlemen who appeared to be in their late fifties, walked in, accompanied by a stunningly beautiful young lady. Introductions were made and we all sat down around the table.

The Douglas Brothers Bakery, I would soon learn, was actually an off-shoot of a business that had been started by their father Alfred. He had opened a small neighborhood bakery in 1947, which gradually grew into a small factory. But the company had really begun to boom only when his three sons took it over in the sixties, after he retired. These three brothers quickly managed to transform this small, family bakery into the most successful and lucrative production bakery in the City.

John, the oldest brother, was the president of the company, and had the most business sense of the three. He had a knack for knowing how to capitalize on emerging markets, and how to leverage success in one area into diverse endeavors. Marty, the middle brother, was the dreamer, the idea man in charge of sales and marketing. And Rupert, the youngest brother, was in charge of production and distribution. Together, these three personalities had complemented each other perfectly, and their collective dynamism allowed them to transform a start-up family business into a corporate behemoth that produced and distributed baked goods to virtually every restaurant and supermarket in the metropolitan area. Well, very impressive, you say. But what exactly does this have to do with your manuscript?

Which is exactly what I asked the brothers when they had finished their self-congratulatory opus.

"Well Dave", John began, "you are probably wondering how we got a hold of your manuscript in the first place. My daughter Nancy, here, works as an editor for St. Mark's Press, a publisher that you had submitted your book proposal to. I'll let her explain."

"I'm employed as an associate editor by St. Mark's", Nancy began. "Part of my job is to review unsolicited proposals, like yours, to determine whether they have any market value. We have a number of junior editors who sift out any of the really worthless junk, but still, ninety percent of the proposals that cross my desk aren't publishable.

Your proposal was something different. And although it was a little rough - it's obvious that you are not a professional writer - to me, that made it refreshing and honest. And I loved the whole idea of a modern Utopian novel. My father will tell you that I talked about it for weeks to anyone willing to listen.

Unfortunately for you, my senior editors would not. They felt that the book was too unusual a genre for today's market, and refused to consider it."

But after listening to my daughter describe it", John chimed in, "I became interested in it myself. And so, after discussing it with my brothers, I asked you to come here to talk to us about it. We'd like to read the full manuscript if you would permit us, to see how it fits in with what we had been planning to do ourselves. But as you have probably surmised by now, we have no interest, or ability for that matter to publish your book. We have something entirely different in mind for you."

"The three of us have made a fortune with this business", Marty continued. "We have also done extraordinarily well with our investments over the last several years. And we have always wanted to be able to give something back to this City which has provided us with so much prosperity. We've donated countless dollars to charities and schools, but the "return" on these investments has always been disappointing to say the least. Like you, we are sick of seeing people living in such appalling conditions in the slums. The real shame is that there are a lot of principled people who live in these areas who are trapped, or at least perceive themselves to be trapped, by the circumstances of their relative poverty. But it seems to us that even in these tough economic times – or especially because of the economy – it is vital for this country to find ways to help lift people out of these cycles of poverty".

"People and families are hurting right now. We want to do something to help out," Rupert continued. "Our idea, much like the model you outlined in your book proposal, is to purchase a group of properties, either abandoned or existing tenements, and renovate them. Once we own them, we will be able to control who lives in them and how they are operated. Interestingly enough, the slow economy and the collapse of the housing market actually provides a unique opportunity for us. We feel that if we can purchase enough of the housing units concentrated in one area, we can establish a thriving neighborhood similar to the one you described."

"So what you are saying is that you actually want to build *Dave's Utopia*? I asked incredulously.

Well, not exactly!" John chuckled. "But close enough. We'll have to start small, though. It's going to take some time to gear up and get things going. And though we are wealthy, we don't have nearly the kind of resources that are needed to build an entire neighborhood. We are going to need some help. Marty is already working on that."

"I've set up a non-profit corporation called the Lucia Foundation", Marty explained. "I've got an interesting idea that I've been batting around with our attorneys, and I think it may be feasible to use both the non-profit Lucia Foundation in concert with a for-profit Real Estate Investment Trust (REIT). "We're using the REIT as an investment vehicle, because we have this wild idea that we can provide an urban renewal model that will actually turn a profit. And once we are able to prove that we can do this, watch out! Everybody and his brother is going to want to copy us. But that will be a good thing."

"We'll use the two organizations to solicit donations and investment capital from local corporations and acquaintances around town. While there will be no minimum donations for the non-profit, investment in the REIT, will require a minimum investment - enough equity to purchase and restore one dwelling unit. As soon as we develop our master plan and enough capital is amassed, we'll begin purchasing properties. This will have to be done gradually, in the strictest secrecy, probably with shadow corporations, so that any land owners in the area don't begin to suspect what we are up to and jack up their prices. And once the neighborhood begins to be established, a governing board, composed of Foundation members will need to oversee the whole operation."

"But this neighborhood will have to be more than just housing", Rupert added. "We want this neighborhood to be a true mixed-use community. In addition to retail, multi-family and office space, there needs to be open space, schools, churches, youth centers, and other civic institutions that will be integrated into the community over time. The streets will need to be pedestrian-friendly, vibrant, and inviting. Landscaping and signage will need to support a sense of place."

"There are also utility, public works, and infrastructure issues that will need to be approved and coordinated with the City, since we are not trying to establish our own independent city-state. I'm going to set up a meeting with the Mayor and the City Attorney as soon as we have identified a site and are ready to begin. The politics of this venture will be like driving a camel through the eye of a needle, so we are going to have to get the backing and cooperation of some key City officials well in advance."

And so we began to discuss the game plan for implementation. After grilling me for about two hours, they then began to debate amongst themselves. How could it be financed and how much start-up capital would be needed? What kind of integration into the existing City services would be required? What kind of political influence would need to be exerted? Could or should we get any state or federal tax credits? Could City Tax Increment Financing (TIFs) be used to build some of the infrastructure and street improvements? Would it be prudent to even raise the issue? What sort of security mechanisms would need to be put in place to protect the initial residents? And on and on.

I spent most of the day in that room. At one time lunch was ordered and then passed around as we continued to talk. Regretfully, Nancy had to leave at noon to get back to her job, but the conversation continued on until nearly five o'clock.

At one point, John suddenly realized something, turned to me and said," Dave, I guess we should have asked you this earlier, but....Do you want to work with us on this?"

"Are you kidding me?!?" I replied "I've been waiting for this my entire adult life!"

It was decided that John and I would work together in identifying a prospective site and outlining the scope of work of the various phases of construction. John and Rupert would help me develop community covenants and leasing agreements. Marty would handle the financing through the Lucia Foundation and the REIT. He would also work with me in developing a master plan for the community as we began filling in the missing pieces.

Rupert would initially act as a liaison between the Douglas Brothers and the City, but would later become the de facto Owner of record, as CEO of the REIT and Director of the Foundation, when the project moved into the construction phase.

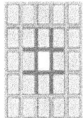

The Plan

And so I was hired to help find a suitable site to make my mythical community into a reality. My new job would be to coordinate the design and construction of the community, and to act as a liaison between the Lucia Foundation and the other parties who would be contracted to do the work. The Brothers also expected me to prepare preliminary plans and building elevations that would be presented to other architects for development into construction documents, and to observe the progress and scrutinize the payments for any building under construction.

I was given a salary that nearly doubled my previous one, and was given free rein to hire on advisors, architects, and engineers, (though The Brothers had definite opinions on whom these advisors, architects and engineers should be). A small office across from the bakery was set up as my temporary architectural office - until an office could be located within our target community. Oftentimes, one or another of the Brothers would pop in unexpectedly to monitor my progress. I would report back to them formally, however, once a week. Nancy, too, would occasionally visit the office to see how things were going, and before long, she became an official member of the management team, a development that I was not at all displeased about.

The first thing that we needed to do, though, was to find a suitable site. In discussions with The Brothers, it was decided that a twenty to thirty square block area would be the ideal size to target for the overall boundaries of the community. An area this size would house enough people to achieve the momentum we would need to expand outward, would provide a large enough population to support a local school district, and most importantly, it would be small enough to defend. It was also the largest area of real estate that could be realistically acquired - even with the immense resources that were quickly being developed through The Lucia Foundation and the REIT. Of course, initially, we would be dealing with at most, a single block. But we felt that we had to develop a master plan for the whole area before we could do anything, and we wanted to think on a grand scale before we identified our first buildings so that we did not encounter unforeseen obstacles later on.

In our initial weekly meetings, we discussed the various phases of development that needed to be orchestrated. Phase I was, as I said, was the identification of the overall site and the purchase of the initial properties. During Phase I the housing stock would be rented out just as they had been by the previous landlords, but we would secretly evaluate the tenants to see if there were any that we wanted to evict.

Phase II was the gradual purchase of the remaining properties within the area of the master plan. As we purchased more and more properties, we would approach the individuals or families we wanted to keep and offer them a chance to enlist in the new community. Those that wished to stay were asked to assist in the renovation effort of a building in return for a rent-to-own agreement that I will speak of later. The renovation effort ultimately became the means by which we were able to weed out the undesirables.

Once we had enough buildings to pull it off, we could shuffle our good tenants into vacant apartments while a particular building was being completely renovated. And we were able to expel the undesirables once their lease expired by simply refusing to offer them a co-op agreement in the building being renovated.

Once Phase II was complete, Phase III involved the renovation and restoration of all of the remaining buildings, and the colonizing of the neighborhood. At this point, we would begin to have more apartments than we had tenants, and would need to start bringing residents in from outside our existing pool of renters. During this phase, a screening process was developed to identify the applicants who would best serve the goals of our community.

Phase IV involved the integration of institutions like banks, schools, churches, etc. into the community and under community control. During this phase, block leaders were elected, security means and methods were introduced, and a community review board was established. This board, which later evolved into our Board of Magistrates, let the residents themselves determine who would be allowed to reside in their community. The establishment of block leaders put a local governing authority in place that allowed the residents to set up community events, services, and allocate resources. This was the first step in making the community self-sufficient and self-responsible.

Phase V, the final phase of development, would be the expansion outward, beyond the initial blocks.

In our weekly meetings the Douglases and I talked for hours on end about all of the facilities that each of us believed would be necessary. John, Marty, Rupert, and Nancy had by now read the full manuscript of my book, and they added their own ideas, wish lists, and criticisms to what I had contributed. As the five of us debated the issues, we were quickly arriving at a consensus of the essential elements of our community.

> **Security:** This was by far, the most important ingredient in this community. If security failed, all else would follow suit. So we devised some parameters for creating areas of defensible space and for securing our boundaries, and came up with the idea of around-the-clock community policing with resident Sentries. We petitioned the City to allow us to close off a number of our streets to through traffic and to place gate posts into each "mini-neighborhood" thus created. We also decided that we

would need a central command post that could rally the entire community into action in the event of an emergency. This later evolved into our Watch Tower.

Education: We believed that it would be important for this community to eventually have its own independent school, since the public school system was abominable. We wanted this school to be patterned on some of the more successful private, preparatory schools in and around the City. After much research, and discussions with City officials, we realized that the only way to achieve what we wanted was to establish a charter school that would serve this neighborhood. After an incredible struggle with the City, the State, the Feds, the NEA, the local school board and PTA, and on and on, we were finally able to open The Academy. Another guiding principal of this community would be to attempt to provide all residents, including adults, with minimum reading, writing and math standards. It was felt that voluntary continuing education classes could benefit all of our residents.

Utilities: We wanted our community to be as self-sufficient as possible. We also were intensely focused on making our homes, businesses and public buildings as environmentally responsible as possible. As corporate sponsors began to get involved in the project, they often wanted to try out new technologies that they were developing on a large urban scale. All of these forces came together in the form of The Furnace, our central utilities plant.

Church: This was probably the most contentious issue that we discussed. Most of us felt that a spiritual center of one form or another would be essential to the community. Though there were any number of existing nearby churches, temples, mosques, etc. in the immediate area, we wanted to discourage our residents from segregating themselves into factions based upon religious identity. Such fragmentation would dilute the whole feeling of community that we were trying to develop. What we really wanted, was a spiritual meeting place that would allow all residents to attend services together. The problem was how to decide what faith, if any, would be represented. If only one faith was sanctioned, this would certainly alienate the residents of other faiths. The obvious solution was to establish an inter-faith church where all faiths were welcome. And since we also did not want to antagonize the existing faith-based organizations that were performing much needed and appreciated charitable work in the area, our idea was to invite a different priest, pastor, rabbi, etc. to deliver the service each week. This was the basis behind which The Rectory was established. However, it proved to be difficult to lure a visiting religious leader as frequently as we wished, and eventually we evolved our services to do without outsiders.

Recreation: Constant activity and involvement, we felt, was the way to avoid many of the problems that plagued other urban communities. Healthy bodies have healthy minds. We needed some sort of recreation center where people could pursue athletic interests, as well as hobbies and vocational training. And we would need a place to house the administrative offices for the Foundation and its staff. These requirements melded together to form the building that we now refer to as simply The Center.

Communication: There were a number of reasons for installing a computer network that linked all of our properties. The ability for the residents to communicate quickly with one another and to our security infrastructure would be vital to the operation of the community. A computer network of high-speed telephone and data lines all tied to a central command post and file server was essential in being able to set up the kind of security measures that we were looking for. We also wanted computers in every residence so that students of all ages would have access to the Internet, and so residents could communicate with one another, and our community governing board via e-mail. But we really wanted computers in every home so that our residents would get accustomed to using them, since we would be trying to educate and train people who lived within our community to acquire skills that would enable them to get higher paying white collar jobs. And so the cost for a computer workstation was built into the price of all of our rent-to-own apartments.

A small, neglected section of the City, five blocks in each direction, was eventually identified for our project. It was ideal because it fit our area requirement, and because the City owned a large percentage of the real estate within it - mostly abandoned, burned out shells and vacant lots. It was an area of the City that had long been neglected, but it had once been an upscale, thriving, urban center. There was a good mix of walkup residences, warehouses, storefronts, and even a scattering of privately-owned detached houses, although most of the buildings were now either abandoned, or else being used as crack houses. The place really needed a great deal of work to make it fit for habitation. The good news was that because of their deteriorated condition and the depressed housing market, the cost to purchase them was going to be quite low. And once they were restored and renovated they showed promise of being truly spectacular buildings - diamonds in the rough.

Rupert felt that once the REIT owned a majority of the usable property, we could persuade the City to sell us the rest. By this time, Marty had coaxed quite a few local philanthropists, businessmen, entertainers, and professional athletes, to join the Lucia Foundation. A number of shadow corporations were set up - one for each building that was targeted - and we began purchasing buildings as they came on the market. At other times, unsolicited offers were proffered to the existing owners of the buildings. At the same time, Rupert began schmoozing the politicians and laying the groundwork for the purchase of the City-owned land. For me, this stage of the process was the most painful - waiting for the acquisition of the neighborhood, and being forced to play the role of slumlord until the time was ripe for the next phase of development to commence.

In the meantime, I spent my days drawing up plans for the buildings that had been acquired, in anticipation of their eventual use. I also worked with John to formulate admission guidelines for future applicants into the community, and worked with Marty and individual Foundation members to set up corporate sponsorships. These sponsorships would become invaluable, later on, in the form of product donations, research and development, and mentoring and employment opportunities for our residents. Due to these contacts, which were forged early on with various industry leaders, The Tope would become sort of a proving ground for many products that a particular corporation wished to put into the marketplace.

Many companies that formed alliances with the Foundation would soon discover that The Tope provided unique opportunities to them as an urban test market; and consequently, we would often receive donations from these companies of a product or device that had not yet been made available to the general public. But more of that later.

After roughly five years of waiting, it was decided that we had enough property to actually start colonizing it. As Rupert predicted, the City agreed to sell their holdings to us. While it might seem surprising at first glance that the City would willing to part with this property, when you consider that we were proposing to develop vacant, and therefore non-revenue producing real estate, into tax producing affordable housing, it was really a win-win situation for the local politicians – and they jumped at it. By the time that the first wave of settlers started moving in, the REIT and the Lucia Foundation owned about ninety percent of the property within the designated twenty-five blocks. By the end of the following year, we owned it all.

Phase III was ready to begin.

The Homesteaders

The process of populating the community was by far the most critical in ensuring that it would prosper. One of the reasons that The Tope works so well is that we have built in a number of mechanisms and safety checks that allow us to keep negative influences from coming in and allow us to purge them when they are encountered inside. But these mechanisms could only function properly if the mix of people that we started out with were overwhelmingly decent, hard-working souls. The people who constituted this first group would be tested to their limits; so we developed an elaborate screening process to help us choose people whom we believed were up to the challenge and whose inclusion would add value to the whole community.

The first wave of settlers, or Homesteaders, as we now call them, had to be a tough, durable bunch - a group of survivors. It was also a requirement that all members of an applicant family be free of drugs and possess no recent criminal record of any significance. Valuable skills, especially in the building or home maintenance fields were considered by us to be a big plus. Former military men and women were also given preference, because they were used to working rigorously in a team atmosphere, a trait that would be essential in the first settlement. Married, two parent families were preferred, although those who were single mothers, single fathers, or just plain single were selected if they had the will and the right attitude. And because we set the marriage preference as a stated goal, an interesting phenomenon started to manifest itself. We began to get more and more applications from couples who were engaged or newly married. I think that as the word got out and people realized that there was actually an advantage to getting married, more and more people became inclined to do so and to apply for their apartment as a family. On the other hand, we did not discriminate against anybody based solely upon their household makeup. As long as we felt that they could add to the success of the community as a whole, they were in.

But from the beginning, we were making it evident that we would try to foster and encourage stable family environments through our policies. The old welfare system, as many recall, had the unintended effect of breaking up families, and encouraging single mothers to have more and more children, even though they could not support their current ones. In many urban areas, the father became irrelevant, since the single mother was given so many benefits from the local, state, and federal government that the father was no longer needed as a provider. This was done, our politicians always told us, in the best interest of the children.

We in The Tope, on the other hand, believe the best interest of the children lies in making two parent households not only a viable alternative, but the preferred family unit. This is not to say that two parent households are always the best; there will always be cases where a broken marriage is better for every individual member of a family - in instances where there is abuse, constant fighting, or infidelity. In The Tope however, childbirth out of wedlock and divorce (especially if children are involved), though legal, are frowned upon - social badges of dishonor. As a result, young women in The Tope tend to be much more careful in their sexual relations than their counterparts elsewhere in the City.

Conversely, stable marriages in The Tope are honored, and fatherhood is exalted. In other parts of the City, young men brag to each other about their "trophies" - the children they have fathered, usually out of wedlock and by as many different women as possible. Rarely are such children supported in any way by these men. Here in The Tope, the only trophies we have are the ones that are given out each year to parents who have demonstrated extraordinary involvement with their children or their community.

Now that is something to brag about!

Choosing the initial Homesteaders was a little bit like the old shipwreck dilemma, only in reverse. Instead of having 20 people from which 10 had to be thrown overboard in order to save the rest, we had thousands of people at sea from which we had to select 5,000 to bring onto the boat, so that we could start to save everyone. Obviously we wanted to get the best mix of people that we possibly could. On the other hand, we didn't want to be accused of elitism, racism or bigotry of any kind. This process had to be one that was accessible to anyone who was willing to put forth the effort, or the larger population would never accept it. But more importantly, that was the right way to do it.

The procedure that we eventually came up with was for applicant families or individuals to be interviewed by three Foundation members, who would then give a yes or no vote. An applicant qualified if they received at least two votes from the interview. Applicants with three votes were immediately accepted into the community. The remaining applicants would then be selected by a lottery system from the pool of these pre-qualified applicants. But the way that we got such a tremendous initial response was remarkably simple. We advertised rental apartments at rates far below the current market rate. We also made a deal with the City - as a condition of our real estate purchase agreement from them - whereby families on public assistance would be allowed to apply for membership in our community.

You see, the City had purchased these properties with the intent of converting them to public-assistance housing, but various factions within the City government had battled for years over the correct way to approach the rebuilding of this neighborhood. And in the end, nothing was done. That is, until we came along. We explained to any new families or individuals who were interested that we were going to pre-qualify applicants for membership in a new community and that if an individual or family pre- qualified, their name would be placed in a pool from which any openings would be randomly assigned. Gradually the word got out on the street as to what we were up to, and at that point, the response was overwhelming. This was something we were completely unprepared for - the hunger of those living in the depressed areas to find a way out, and the willingness to try anything in order to get out.

Instead of traditional rental contracts, we were offering these units as rent-to-own cooperative homes. Each building had been purchased as I've mentioned, through a shadow corporation, financed by the REIT or through donations to the Foundation. During our weekly meetings, Marty had strenuously argued that the residents must be given the opportunity to own the homes that they lived in, since pride of ownership would be an important theme in keeping the community flourishing. Although the rest of our team agreed with him in principle, we couldn't allow the ownership of these homes to be simply a hand-out, especially since the investors in the REIT were expecting a return on their investment. We eventually agreed upon a system whereby ownership of the apartments would be earned through a combination of hard work, dedication and monthly payments - and a framework was devised to monitor the efforts of the individual Homesteaders.

Initial profits from the Foundation investments were used to purchase additional real estate when the community expanded. So for the units that were purchased by the non-profit, the original investment had to be regarded as seed money rather than as an investment or conversely, a gift, or this community would never be taken seriously by outsiders. And for the REIT properties, if we could show that a profit could be made while renovating an area as badly deteriorated as this, it would be much easier to obtain support when we, or someone following our model, expanded into other urban areas, or other cities. Furthermore, and perhaps most importantly, the Homesteaders themselves would never feel true pride of ownership if the homes were merely handed over to them - it was essential that they be earned legitimately through their own efforts.

It was our objective to find a plausible method to allow this to be accomplished; a method that would make home ownership and family stability the path of least resistance. To really understand The Tope, it's important to keep in mind that we were not simply building a neighborhood. In actuality, we were putting in place a process - a series of guidelines, rules of conduct, and contractual agreements that were tied to institutions, and community-based programs. The buildings themselves were merely the vessels needed to carry this process through to fruition.

We wanted the community to function as a kind of self-perpetuating mechanism. Once a fertile site, good people, and a set of ground rules were put in place, The Tope, it is hoped, should be able to be replicated within any city in the country. And given enough time it should eventually spread outward until it consumes the rest of the decaying slum around it.

But let's get back to the rental agreements. We started by determining the average building value of all the buildings within the twenty-five square blocks, including the estimated cost of all renovation work and the purchase price. We had to do it this way because the condition of the buildings varied so much. Some needed only cosmetic repairs. Most of them though, especially those purchased from the City, were in much worse shape, requiring almost total gutting and rebuilding. Often a building was nothing more than a boarded up facade in front of a vacant lot. And so obviously the cost of renovation varied greatly from building to building.

Once an average building cost was determined, we were able to come up with an average square foot cost, which we used to determine the cost of a typical 1,000 square foot, two bedroom apartment. Larger or smaller apartments would be pro-rated accordingly from this baseline. We then calculated the monthly payment that would need to be made by the resident in order to pay for their apartment, assuming a thirty year loan with current available interest rates. This would be the base rent of that apartment. Each family renting the apartment would sign a loan agreement with the Foundation for their space, and would in turn receive shares in a co-op every time they paid their rent in full.

However, there was one small catch. Most of the families moving in did not generate enough income to pay the full rent. As a result, they would be required to earn their shortfall in other ways. For instance, all families were required to assist in the renovation of one of our buildings before they were allowed to move into their own home site. Everybody above the age of sixteen was required to participate in some way. This effort reduced the square foot cost of the apartment and provided the family with a bank of hours that would prevent them from defaulting on their loan for the immediate future. Once they moved in, families could also receive credit toward their rent by performing any number of community service assignments handed down by their block leaders.

In terms of the renovation effort, we wanted to use this as an opportunity to teach a trade to anyone who was so inclined. As a result, whenever we negotiated a contract with a general contractor to perform work on any of our buildings, we insisted that the contractor also serve as a mentor for any of our residents who were willing to sign on as apprentices. On the surface, this would seem to be a tremendously more expensive method to renovate a building. But since our corporate sponsors donated a lot of the building materials, the costs tended to balance out. And over time, we developed a trained resident workforce of plumbers, electricians, framers, masons, drywallers, painters etc. that lowered our subsequent costs dramatically. Some of these workmen eventually became so skilled that they started up their own companies and began to bid on subsequent renovation projects. This process also achieved two other goals. It allowed many of our residents to receive training in a trade that enabled them to get good paying jobs elsewhere. It also allowed us as a community to gradually build up a skilled building maintenance workforce and a stock house of construction equipment. This equipment, which we allowed Homesteaders to check-out at any time, was stored in a large maintenance room in a formally abandoned warehouse that eventually became our power plant, The Furnace.

The home sites themselves range from studio and one-bedroom apartments, which are well suited to the elderly and our young, single "Urbanistas", to four and five bedroom floor-thrus for larger families, as well as a small number of detached houses. There is a great deal of diversity in unit layouts, space allocation and even craftsmanship. We wanted to avoid the cookie cutter approach that characterizes most public housing, since we believe that it leads to a complacency of personal initiative and a unity of despair. We wanted a certain degree of envy and discontent to develop, as long as there were means available to act positively on those emotions. So we put in place some rules that would allow families to sell their units back to the Foundation and acquire a better model, if they could afford to pay a slightly higher monthly payment. The key was that they had to work for it through their own initiative. Many families took advantage of this by finding additional employment, or by starting up small home businesses.

Since in most instances we were starting from scratch, we had great flexibility in laying out the spaces. This enabled us to integrate a number of technological gadgets that are critical to our security, and enabled us to include some building components, inventions and new appliances (which some of our corporate sponsors wanted us to test for them) that are not normally included in urban residences. It also allowed us to design the layouts for the buildings, mostly three and four story walk-ups, in a way that would complement the other security measures that we were putting in place for the residents, and allow them to assert a certain degree of control over their immediate surroundings.

We drew greatly from the work and teachings of Oscar Newman, the architect who almost single-handedly pioneered the concept of "Defensible Space" in public housing. Defensible Space concepts use building form, circulation patterns, landscaping features such as fencing, planting beds, play areas, etc., and even site lighting to create small mini-neighborhoods within a larger development, and areas of territoriality that tend to minimize places where anonymous criminal activity can occur. Defensible space programs also rely on the residents themselves to assert their control over these spaces and thus aim to mitigate governmental involvement in building upkeep and criminal enforcement within the targeted area. These principles fit in well with the guiding values that The Tope was founded upon.

Lastly, our need to build from the ground up enabled us to design the housing to suit the specific needs of the families who were moving into them. If a family needed an extra bedroom or had accessibility requirements for a handicapped family member we accommodated that specific need. It seemed impractical to us to make every home in a building, or even a fixed percentage of them, handicapped accessible, when we could easily adapt our plans as required. You see we didn't ignore the needs of people with special needs, we just responded to them on a case by case basis, and thus with greater efficiency and care.

Each Block, for instance, was required to set aside a number of temporary housing units for the homeless and mildly mentally disabled. As altruistic we would have liked to be, however, we had to set firm limits on the number of these units, or we foresaw ourselves being suffocated by an infusion of indigents. There was a delicate balance, as we saw it, between addressing a problem and perpetuating the problem. We tried to select individuals or families for these temporary units that were truly in need of a hand to get them back on the right track - not those that were just looking for a handout.

Our "adopted" families and individuals tend to be cared for much more intelligently and humanely in a community such as this, than they would be in a shelter or psychiatric hospital or out on the streets. Here, they are free to come and go as they please, but they know that they always have a roof over their head, and they are watched over by all of the families that live on that particular block. In exchange for their lodging, they are required, as are all of the Homesteaders, to participate in community service projects, and are required to secure some form of employment within three months of their arrival. Nobody gets a free ride in The Tope. Those with substance abuse problems are also required to take part in a therapy program sponsored by the community and administered in our Infirmary. And those with physical or mental disabilities are assisted by resident volunteers in their attempt to secure employment.

Single homeless men and women are often given a group apartment so that they can, as a group, afford to pay the rent, even though, individually, they are paying only a small portion. Bank accounts are set up for these individuals at the S & L, and clothing and toiletries, donated by the other residents, allow them to present themselves favorably to prospective employers. Many homeless families and individuals have assimilated into the community so well that nobody realizes any more that they were once so down on their luck. Likewise, many marginally mentally impaired individuals have learned skills that are useful to the community and have become integral participants in our small society.

As we got into the actual restoration process we established rules for the amount of time that every individual was required to put in before the family as a whole was allowed to receive its space. Everybody chipped in though. Some did carpentry, some learned how to do plumbing or electrical work, and some painted or put down tile. Others were put in charge of landscaping and street beautification.

Many of the Homesteaders never got that interested or involved in construction at all. However, that didn't mean that they didn't help out in other ways. There was plenty of work that was needed, and not all of it hammering and sawing. Many people fulfilled their work requirement by working in our administrative offices, doing bookkeeping, filing, etc. And in so doing, they reduced our administrative overhead while learning valuable office skills. Some chose to help me out in the planning and construction office that was established on site and were able to get first-hand experience in the design, computer drafting, engineering and business aspects of the construction industry.

Still others fulfilled their requirement by acting as day care supervisors - watching young children while parents were working at a construction site, or assisted our doctors in The Infirmary. Finally, a number of people chose to assist the elderly residents of our community, a process that eventually evolved into our Nightingale program that I will speak of later.

My personal favorite though was a group of teenagers who got together with one of our corporate sponsors, a large chemical company. These young men and women became experts at restoring and cleaning the facades of our buildings. And they have become an essential tool in the restoration effort. Although we refer to them now as anti-graffiti artists, or Aggies for short, they do much more than remove graffiti. They are experts in all kinds of stone and masonry restoration, paint removal (especially lead-based paint), and wood repair. Our corporate sponsor was so pleased with the results of the Aggies' work that it donated the now omnipresent Aggie bomber jackets. These jackets have become such a status symbol in The Tope that every teenager wants to become an Aggie. But it is much tougher now than it was originally to be selected for A.G. duty; now only the best chemistry students are allowed into the group.

But I'm getting ahead of myself!

Although slow at first, the restoration effort got easier and easier with each new building we tackled, as our pool of skilled workers grew. We began to develop a trained construction workforce, and in the long run this made our community far less dependent upon outside help. In the short term, people learned and continue to learn valuable skills that they can in turn bring to the marketplace. Working with one's own hands to produce something of lasting worth and beauty also tends to raise one's self esteem and leads to a pride of ownership. And because of this, our Homesteaders are far less apt to destroy their environment, or to allow it to be destroyed by others. They are proud of what they have built. It has become a part of them, and they will protect it and defend it to their dying breath.

Lastly, the restoration effort resulted in a kind of esprit de corps, amongst all the Homesteaders. We required a lot out of a family in order for it to become eligible for a home in The Tope and its obligations continue after the family moves in, as part of the rent-to-own contract. Those who make it have the bond of going through a common experience, almost like boot camp in the military. In addition, many of the established families help out when a new home site is being built, even though they aren't required to do so. It becomes a social event, akin to the Amish barn raising, that allows the new-comers to get to know the families that they will be living with, and vice versa.

As you are probably beginning to see, positive solutions, when implemented together, start to build upon one another. Buckminster Fuller, the great American architect, engineer, and inventor, coined the term "synergy" to describe this phenomenon. Synergy, he explained, results when two or more forces working together, produce unexpected effects that are greater than they could have achieved individually. We are beginning to see such synergistic effects in our community. As we begin to solve one problem, it unexpectedly leads to solutions in other areas that are seemingly unrelated.

Several months back, as I was tending to my tomato plants on the rooftop, I heard an elderly woman explain to her grandson how to raise a healthy and prosperous garden. "First you need to plant the seeds in good soil and give them plenty of nourishment and light in order for them to start growing. As they start to grow, you need to protect them and pick out any weeds that might have blown in. 'Cause one bad weed can take hold and spread like wildfire. And before you know it that weed will strangle your whole garden. Once your plants start to grow you can put in stakes and tie them to it. This will force the plant to grow straight and tall. After a time you can remove the stakes, once the plant has enough strength to grow on its own."

As I listened to her I realized that she could have been talking just as easily about raising a child in The Tope. What we have done here in The Tope is to create a community with those same guiding principles. We have provided a place where good people can flourish. We have forces in place that help to keep the "weeds" out, and mechanisms to remove "weeds" that sprout from within. We provide incentives for people to follow a decent way of life, and enforce severe penalties for those who break the rules. The rules are simple and the penalties are known to all. And justice is always swift and impartial. That's the way it's supposed to be in America.

 Some people will complain that our community has merely created another class system within the current class system, and that thus our approach is patently unfair. They will say that our success is due to the fact that we are helping out only those who are the easiest to help and that we have turned our backs on the most difficult cases. What can I say? All of these charges are true. But I don't see this as an indictment of our community. Instead, I see it as a measure of our success.

To try to lift up everybody all at once, equally and steadily, is impossible and idiotic. It cannot be done. And yet we have been trying to do just that in our inner cities for the last forty years. We cannot help everybody – only those who have the will to help themselves. But isn't that the American way?

The Bouncers

By now you must be wondering how decisions are made in The Tope and how they are implemented. Although initially, all decisions were made by the board of the Lucia Foundation, we gradually shifted more and more responsibilities to an elected community governing board.

The residents of every Block elect a Block Chairman. We call these elected representatives "Bouncers" for some reason; nobody is quite sure where this term came from anymore, but the name stuck, and it is the name that everybody now uses. The Bouncers are primarily responsible for seeing to the day-to-day needs of the Block and are also responsible for seeing that every resident of the Block performs his or her requisite tasks. Since it would be quite impossible for one individual to handle all of this, the Bouncer usually delegates responsibilities to deputies of his or her own choosing. Once selected as a deputy, a person is obligated to serve as requested. But usually, the Bouncer picks people who are known to be willing, as well as enthusiastic and competent.

The deputies perform a variety of functions. For instance, there is one person on each Block who is in charge of security; and that deputy sets up the roster for Sentry duty, makes sure that all of the surveillance equipment is in good repair, organizes self-defense classes, etc. There is likewise another deputy in charge of building repair and maintenance, another in charge of Block social activities, and so on. The Bouncer is free to appoint any number of deputies with any number of duties, at his own discretion. And all of the deputies meet with the Bouncer at a weekly meeting to go over status reports and future business.

Once a month, all residents of a particular Block meet - usually in either The Rectory or a classroom in The Academy, and discuss any issues that need to be voted upon. Usually these meetings are preceded by a sort of potluck block party, so they tend to be raucous, informal events that everybody looks forward to. The Bouncer always prepares an agenda for each meeting that is distributed via e-mail a few days prior to the meeting; and during the meeting, the Bouncer leads the discussion, presents all the issues, and calls for the vote.

Sometimes a show of hands is all that is needed, but at other times, especially when the more controversial or important issues are discussed, the vote is taken electronically over the Internet, after the meeting, so that everyone is given the chance to vote. Every resident above the age of sixteen is allowed to vote, and majority rules. And every year, an election is held to either retain or appoint a new Bouncer. We have no term limits for these positions, since we believe that if a person is doing the job well there is no reason for change; and if a person is doing the job badly, he or she can be removed by popular vote at the next election.

Every fourth month, all of the Bouncers get together and discuss any issues that are pertinent to the community as a whole. They also elect a community President, once a year, who presides over all of the other Bouncers, and they nominate individuals to be elected into the Board of Magistrates, the judicial wing of the community government. Once any community-wide issues are ready to be voted upon, they are brought back and presented to the individual Blocks at the next Block meeting by their respective Bouncer and voted upon electronically and tallied by the central computer system in The Center. The result of the vote is broadcast by the President to every voter via mass e-mail.

I'm often asked by people who first hear about The Tope, what we do to prevent our leaders from becoming corrupt. I usually respond that we have no leaders, only representatives. You see we don't see our political offices as being full-time jobs, and so our representatives are expected to work and contribute to the daily menial chores that need to be done, just like everybody else. There is no pay involved, and few if any perks. And although Bouncers tend to be the most respected and admired individuals within a particular Block, it is not because of the title. Rather, it is because they are admired and respected that they are given the position in the first place.

The real answer to the question, though, is that we have set it up so that there is very little to be gained by being corrupt, because our representatives have very little actual power - other than the power to influence those that they represent through reason. Also, our Bouncers are so closely involved in the daily life of the community and so immediately culpable to the people they represent, that any impropriety is likely to be noticed. In the final analysis, our local government works because everybody is involved, has a voice, and has a direct interest in what is at stake. It is a method of representation that many politicians in this country, as well as the general electorate, would do well to emulate. For in order for a representative democracy to function properly, an informed public, and political figures who truly represent them, are both required.

The Board

There is one aspect of life in The Tope that many outsiders find objectionable, but which we find is essential to the operation of our community; that is our policy of banishment. There are several cardinal rules in The Tope. All residents are aware of them and know that if they break one of them they are out of the community permanently – no questions asked and no appeals. For instance, we do not tolerate physical abuse of children or spouses. And if our Board of Magistrates determines that a resident has committed a violent act against a family member, that person is immediately banished from the community; the Sentries are immediately informed, and after that individual is escorted out, he or she is not permitted within our boundaries ever again.

While we encourage the remaining family members to stay within our boundaries, they are of course free to go as well. But if they choose to stay, they have the comfort of knowing they are safe from their assailant within the confines of The Tope. Our Board is neither a criminal nor a civil court of law. Its only power is to enforce the covenants of the community that every settler has assented to through their rent-to-own contract. But the power to expel an individual from the community, by denying that individual the ability to rent or own an apartment within it, is a power that is absolutely essential for us. It enables us to remove the "weeds" that have grown from within. And when a community is able to remove those who do not abide by the commonly held good, it enables the community to flourish in so many other ways.

Our school, The Academy, is a good example of this. You will find no drugs or guns, or weapons of any kind for that matter among our students here, because they all know that if they are caught with drugs or a weapon, they are out of The Tope, and consequently force a terrible decision upon their parents. Interestingly to some, we do not have any zero tolerance rules in our Academy. Our thought on this was that zero tolerance really means zero common sense. For instance, we do not expel students for bringing medication to school if they are not feeling well, and we would never automatically discipline a student for carrying a pocket knife, as long as the knife is used responsibly by that student. Our parents expect our administrators to be pragmatic and to discipline only those whose actions need to be corrected.

To get back to the issue of banishment, though, the implicit threat has led to a kind of positive peer pressure among the school children that prevents the introduction of disturbing influences like drugs and violence. And once safety and behavioral problems have been largely eliminated, it makes it much easier for children to concentrate on learning. But I will speak of this later.

As I've said, selling or purchasing illegal drugs is a "deadly sin" in The Tope. As are acts of prostitution, armed robbery, and the more violent crimes like arson, burglary, rape, homicide, etc. These crimes, while extremely rare in The Tope, are prosecuted in the City criminal court. However, our Board of Magistrates holds its own independent trial and determines whether banishment is required. Because our Board is so efficient, it often reaches a decision before a preliminary hearing is even scheduled in the City courts. We see no reason why we should harbor a felon in our midst while the City plods through an overcrowded docket.

I should also say here that in The Tope, there is no such thing as an attempted crime. By this I mean that an act is judged to be a banishable offense regardless of whether that person succeeded in his effort, or not. To us, it is the intent, not the result that is most important. Why be lenient with someone merely because they bungled the job; it makes no sense whatsoever. And yet this is routinely the way cases are decided in City, State, and Federal Courts.

Of course not all offenses are punishable by banishment. We

residents of The Tope are fallible just like people in any other community. The difference, I think, is that we do not allow our laws to be broken without consequence. We believe that all laws and ordinances are meant to be obeyed. Otherwise, they should not have been enacted in the first place, or they should be amended through the legislative process. We also believe that if minor transgressions are not confronted and corrected, such negligence can lead to an eroding of citizens' respect for the law itself and for those who enforce the law.

Any Homesteader who witnesses a transgression is encouraged to report the incident to the Block Bouncer, who decides whether or not to pass it on to the Board. In addition, the local beat cops are encouraged to report any minor violations they encounter directly to the Bouncer. And all wrongdoing is punished in one way or another. Usually the punishment handed down by the Board is some form of symbolic retribution. Someone caught jaywalking, for instance, must spend a day directing traffic at one of our construction sites. If someone steals from a store, he is forced to pay a fine directly to the store owner. Someone creating a public nuisance is required to deliver a speech of apology at the next Block meeting.

One thing that we don't punish, in any way, however, is speech. Like the founding fathers, we believe that free speech, no matter how offensive or hateful it may seem to others, is essential in a democratic society. We encourage all of our residents, especially our youngest ones, to engage in spirited debate, because we believe that honest discourse is the best way to arrive at consensus and solutions to any problem. We never condemn or prohibit people from having certain beliefs. Instead, we discuss the issues with such wrongheaded people in the arena of public debate. But unless a Homesteader commits an actual offense, we cannot in good conscience punish their thought process.

For offenses where actual damage has been caused to another individual or individual's property, like vandalism or minor assault, the punishment is almost always the same. The offender in these instances is usually forced to become a "slave for the day" and the injured party can use this 'slave' to perform any tasks at all - within certain limits. The "slave for a day" must wear a special uniform (old fashioned prison stripes!) and is treated for the entire day with contempt and derision by the Homesteaders who run across him, although all is forgiven the next day when that person dons his normal attire. While this may seem bizarre to outsiders, this exercise is meant to teach the offender that his actions not only hurt the person whom he had targeted, they also hurt the community as a whole. In a country in which so many young men and women lose their liberty by becoming prisoners – locked up in a cage and forced to do whatever the warden or the prison guards demand them to do - it is a way to provoke our residents into understanding that loss of freedom is the ultimate consequence of living outside the law – of becoming an "outlaw." Conversely, it is meant to demonstrate to the offender that the price of freedom in a representative democracy such as ours, is obedience to the commonly held good. In other words, people are free to do as they choose within the framework of our laws, even to fight to change laws they believe are unjust; but they are not free to pick and choose which laws they will obey.

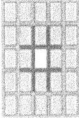

The Savings and Loan

After about three years or so into the settlement of The Tope, we ran into a financial crisis. Our crisis was that The Lucia Foundation, our non-profit corporation, had too much money! Eventually, we would need these funds to purchase additional property outside of our 25 block start-up area, but we were nowhere near being ready to do that. So we needed to either spend our surplus or reinvest it somehow. Another issue that developed was that some of our Homesteaders became interested in starting up small businesses. Several of the buildings that were renovated had ground floor storefronts. We had already rented a lot of these out to merchants, most of whom were not residents of The Tope, but more than half of them remained vacant before our first year concluded.

At about the same time, one of our Urbanistas, Master Jordan, petitioned to fulfill his community obligation by teaching an evening class on entrepreneurialism and had attracted a small group of Homesteaders who were interested in learning how to start-up and run a business. He was assisted in this effort by a number of our retired residents who had owned businesses during their lifetime. Master Jordan was also able to lure a number of the Lucia Foundation members and CEO's from our corporate sponsors to either speak as guest lecturers or act as mentors to individual Homesteaders. And by the time the class was over, most of the students wanted to go out and start up a business of one kind or another. The Bouncers were quite willing to rent out the remaining storefronts to them, but these people needed some start-up capital, and traditional banks would not lend to them.

The final factor that went into our decision to start up an S & L was an agreement among the Bouncers that we should encourage the residents to start some kind of savings plan for retirement. One of the Foundation board members had the ludicrous idea of offering residents matching funds for any money that they were willing to invest in a retirement fund. But the other board members quickly chastised him.

A lot of the surplus, they reminded him, was the result of the initial investment from individual Lucia Foundation members and corporate sponsors. As such, they argued, it was really not ethical to simply give this money away - especially when it had not been earned. Such an action, in any case, though based upon a laudable goal, could be looked upon as a socialist wealth redistribution scheme and was completely inconsistent with the founding principles of The Tope.

And these funds would be needed eventually to purchase additional properties. It would be far better, they argued to invest the surplus in the stock market, bonds, or in the form of business and personal loans, where a return on the investment could be obtained. This could be done in concert with savings accounts for the residents which would offer a return on their savings in the form of a favorable interest payment. And this S & L would provide the residents with the means to obtain a loan without prejudice, since the bank doing the lending would be their bank. The only basis for approving a particular loan is whether the business plan that is presented to the bank is likely to result in a profitable business.

And so, our S & L was established as a publicly owned corporation. Rather than set up traditional savings accounts for our Homesteaders, each individual that contributes money into an account is given shares proportional to the amount invested. In turn, this money is used by the bank manager, in combination with the aforementioned surplus, to provide loans to our local entrepreneurs. And all remaining funds are invested by the manager into a diverse portfolio of stocks and bonds. Each quarter, the success of the overall fund is evaluated by the manager. A percentage of all returning income is rolled back into the surplus fund, while the remaining income is distributed back to the shareholders as a return on their investment. Our bank therefore functions much like the 401K plans to which more affluent individuals have access. The only difference is that a large portion of the fund is reinvested in the local economy. And the local residents who contribute to the plan are able to easily monitor the success of their investment based upon the success of the local entrepreneurs and are more likely to spend their money with the local merchants. This tends to incline the bank manager towards scrupulous review of all of the loan requests, and makes it unlikely that he will approve a loan that is exceedingly risky or unjustifiable. Lastly, it makes the bank manager that much more eager to work with the loan applicants, and allow them to revise their business plan in a way that will most likely lead to a successful start-up business.

In order to start up the Savings & Loan, Master Jordan was enticed into becoming the CEO and bank manager. It has done quite well over the last few years, even in this depressed economy. The stock and bond investments, have also made some modest gains as well; as have most of the businesses started by those Homesteaders who were approved for these entrepreneurial loans. There have been some failures as well, but the positive has outpaced the negative – and even those individuals that failed in their initial enterprises have gained valuable experience in running a business. Several went on to try new ventures with varying degrees of success. Keep in mind that every success story has meant new jobs for our residents and increased tax revenues to the City. And those who were wise enough to begin investing in their retirement account from the beginning are now well on their way to a secure financial future.

The Academy

Well, what have you done about educating your children, you ask? To answer that, I will need to explain the history of our community school and how we fought to establish it and keep it functioning properly. When we first got started building The Tope, we had only a few apartment buildings that were under our control and there were only a handful of families renting from us. But we were looking forward to a day when we would have a population large enough to support a small school district.

Early on, we established a task force that included Marty Douglas and I, several interested residents, and some of our corporate sponsors. We researched all of the possibilities that were available for a small local school. The bureaucracy, regulation, and central control that characterizes most public school systems were the antithesis of the principles by which The Tope was founded. Therefore, a district school within the larger school system was ruled out, since the residents of The Tope would have no control over its operation.

The possibility of a small private school was also examined as well. While this was the most desirable option, it did not make sense financially. Since most of the residents of The Tope were on the lower end of the economic ladder, it was simply not feasible to ask them to pay additional money for schools when they were already paying - through property taxes on their apartments and income taxes from their paychecks - for an ineffective public school system.

At about the same time, the charter school movement sprouted up in several cities across the country. As some of you may already know, a charter school is an independently run school that operates within the larger public school system. Although charter schools receive funding from the locality in which they operate, they have great freedom in designing curricula, hiring and firing teachers, and establishing school policies. Such schools are given a "charter" to operate for a fixed number of years, after which time they are assessed to see if the school has met the educational goals that the charter was based upon. If not, the charter is revoked.

Our task force saw the charter school initiative as being the most promising path for establishing our own school. We researched some of the more successful charter schools that had already been established elsewhere and analyzed the problems associated with some of the failures. In the end, we applied to the state for a charter with the help of a local congresswoman who was championing the charter school initiative in our state, and with the backing of a for-profit company that managed several charter schools in neighboring states.

The main reason for our eventual triumph in obtaining a school charter was, we believe, that our growing population, in an area of the city that had long been mostly abandoned, was creating too great a strain on the outlying public schools. It was coming to the point where an additional school building was absolutely necessary. In order to avoid the political pain associated with redistricting, and the financial pain associated with building a new multi-million dollar school, the city finally caved in and agreed to allow our charter school, as long as our community association (i.e. The Foundation) agreed to pay for the actual facility. An abandoned warehouse in the center of our target community was purchased by the Lucia Foundation and was renovated and converted into classrooms with the help of our Homesteaders over the course of roughly four years.

We decided to call the school, in the Greek philosophic tradition, The Academy. One of our primary goals, from the outset, was to limit class size to fewer than twenty students per teacher. We also wanted to attract quality teachers with relatively high pay scales based upon a "pay for performance" model. To accomplish this, we sought a school administrator who could come up with some innovative solutions. We hired a woman, Master Searles, who had formerly been the headmaster at a small local prep school to run The Academy.

The secret to The Academy's success is very simple - competition. You see The Academy, unbeknownst to anyone who lives outside of The Tope, is really **two** schools that operate in competition with one another under the same roof. Similarly, our children compete with one another on annual tests that are administered by our school. Those scoring in the top ten percent earn a ten percent reduction in rent for their families. Those scoring in the top twenty percent earn a five percent reduction. This tends to get the parents actively involved in motivating their child's educational achievements.

Now I know that "competition" is rapidly becoming anathema in modern public schools. There are classes being taught out there without any grades being given, or else given fallaciously without any link to actual performance. School sports are being organized in which everyone, regardless of ability, gets to play and where score is never kept. All of this is done in the purported interest of raising the child's self-esteem. And that's fine.

Let me rephrase that.

It WOULD be fine if we were living in communist CHINA!

In America, though, such collectivist principles are in direct conflict with the rest of our societal structure. The American capitalist system is rooted in competition and rugged individualism. So why would we want to teach our children that competition is bad and collective advancement is the ideal? Quite the opposite, we have found that competition spurs children to achieve their best and to exert positive peer pressure on themselves to achieve more than is expected of them. Our kids don't need to be taught self-esteem. They need to be taught skills.

In the Academy, we set standards for our children far above the international average. And when you set the bar high, you are often surprised at how many children achieve that high mark. But if you set your sights low, you'll never get any higher. Our children have high self-esteem for the right reasons - because they are accomplishing their goals and learning valuable skills that will continue to help them achieve great things throughout their entire lives. And for us to do any less would be to neglect our moral and professional obligations as educators.

I have seen studies published indicating that schoolchildren in this country suffer on average from an overblown sense of self-esteem. They think they are good at math for instance, even though they test far below the international average. The schoolchildren at The Academy also believe that they are good at math (and reading, writing, oration, science, history, and foreign languages for that matter). But the difference between our children and the average public school student is that our children really are good at those subjects - and have the test scores to prove it! This is because we have developed a school where all teachers and administrators are focused on teaching, and all children are expected to learn.

Master Searles also urged us to abandon the traditional K through 12 grade level structure. She established a new structure based upon 26 gauges of learning, 26 being the lowest gauge and 1 being the highest. Students do not graduate until they reach 1st gauge in several core subject areas. In public schools elsewhere, grade levels are primarily determined by age rather than by the acquisition of skills and knowledge and students are passed through year after year - often graduating from High School without being able to read or perform basic mathematical functions.

The students coming into our school were at remarkably different skill levels - even within the same age group. And the skill levels of an individual child were often vastly different depending upon the subject matter. Therefore, we needed a way to place children with similar levels of learning into the same classes regardless of age. And we needed a way for students to be able to be assigned to their appropriate skill level for each particular area of knowledge. The gauge system made this transition practical.

Under this system, a student might, for instance, attend 14 gauge Math in the first period, 12 gauge English in the second period, 15 gauge History in the third period, and so on. But we didn't assign the gauge numbers. Only the teachers and administrators knew these. Instead, we assigned plant, animal, and mineral names to each class – Ruby Level History, Tiger Level Math, or Maple Level Reading. Since nobody except the teachers and administrators knew what the names meant, there was no resistance from the students or the parents to the assignments once an initial testing and sorting process was completed. And there was no stigma attached in being assigned to a lower or higher gauge for a particular subject.

Although this system was somewhat disorienting at first, over time, most students unknowingly settled into a particular gauge level for the majority of their classes, usually one that was appropriate for their respective age. But the system also allowed more talented individuals to advance at their own rate of learning, while those that had trouble in one subject or another, would not be promoted until they had mastered that area of knowledge. In the end, the majority of the students are happy with this system because it is patently fair and it minimizes the tedium and frustration that was endemic in a school system that forced children into classes that were either too easy or too difficult for them.

But the real challenge was in being able to hire the number of teachers necessary to meet our desired student to teacher ratio with the funds that we had available. The obvious solution was to severely restrict administrative staffing and superfluous school programs. One thing that always shocks visitors to our school, for instance, is the lack of school athletic teams. Now I don't know how it got started out there, but I have to ask you, what in the world does playing football have to do with learning? Not one thing as far as I can see. So we do not have any school sports teams. This doesn't mean that we don't allow our kids to play sports in The Tope. In fact we have more than a few club teams, paid for, coached by, and organized directly by the parents. Some of these teams are quite talented and successful, but they are completely independent of the school system and the school administration. We also do not have a school library or a school librarian, as all children have access to the public library nearby, and all families in The Tope have computers with Internet access.

Likewise, we have no school psychologists or guidance counselors, since these functions are largely handled out of school by either Urbanistas or Homesteaders fulfilling their community obligations. And we have no school nurse. If children feel ill, they are immediately sent next door to the community Infirmary. Many public schools these days use the school psychologists and school nurse mainly to dispense drugs. The over-diagnosis of Attention Deficit and Hyperactivity Disorder and the over-medication of children with mood altering drugs like Ritalin is truly appalling to us. Our children behave in class and excel in their work without such medications. Attentive parents and teachers, a good diet, adequate discipline, and challenging coursework are often all that is needed to correct the behavior of such children.

Instead of a school-run cafeteria, we decided to contract out our food service to a number of vendors who compete with one another for business. Each child receives an account number that they need to memorize, which enables them to spend a certain amount every day on a lunch of their choice. They punch in their account number at the register of their chosen vendor, and the vendor is reimbursed each week based on the number of meals that have been sold.

Parents are able to log into a site to monitor what their kids have been eating at school; and Master Searles and the CEAs periodically review the menus of the various vendors to make sure that they are providing well-balanced meals, and demand changes when necessary.

Although we have no school gymnasium, we utilize the

community Recreation Center next door to give our students a break from their studies. One hour breaks are staggered in three shifts throughout the afternoon, allowing each child to get much needed exercise, eat their lunch or just relax. We find that such a break is essential for children, especially the youngest ones, in keeping them focused in the classroom. But we thought it was ridiculous to incur the expense of a gymnasium, when we had a perfectly adequate facility, only steps away.

Eliminating superfluous and redundant services in our school, frees up funds for the two things that are most important - teaching and learning. In fact, during her first year as headmaster of The Academy, Master Searles hired only two other individuals to help manage the two schools. These two CEA's (Chief Educational Administrators), after consulting with the Headmaster, hired three teachers per gauge for each of their respective schools. In addition to this, one teacher for each gauge was selected by Master Searles to teach classes for especially bright or hard-working children who would be selected on a per subject basis.

After all of the teachers were assigned, each CEA met with their teachers and worked out a curriculum for the year. Then, parents of eligible students, after reviewing the teacher's credentials, were allowed to interview the teachers in an open forum. They were then asked to list the teachers they would prefer their son or daughter to have for a particular subject, in order of preference. Their responses were run through a computer program that sought to match the preferred teacher with that student. From that, classes were filled out accordingly.

The other positive effect that the dual school system has, and one that was quite unexpected to us, is in fostering a sense of friendly competitiveness between students in the two schools. There has developed, over time, a core group of students and their respective parents who believe that the West Wing of the Academy is superior to the East Wing, and vice versa. These two factions, and thus the two schools, compete against each other for better test scores, awards at math and science competitions, etc.

We have found that such competition is a good thing, for it spurs students to put positive peer pressure on others within their respective schools to succeed, and it causes students to push themselves further in their ability to learn than they would otherwise believe possible.

In terms of the curriculum, in the highest gauges, we stick to the fundamentals. The emphasis is on teaching the students to be able to read and write and to understand basic mathematical principles. We do not try to push any belief system onto them – neither liberal nor conservative dogma can be found in our curriculum. We believe that if our children can read, write and do arithmetic, all else will follow in its course. We also stick to tried and true methods of teaching. There is no such thing as team teaching in our schools, and you will never hear the term "new math."

As children move to the lower gauges, we gradually add more and more topics: American and World History, Sciences, Art and Music, Computers, Economics, and Politics. We also teach an elective course in Ethics. And all students, regardless of their gauge, spend every Friday afternoon in either a composition or public speaking class, since these are skills that every professional must have. As we cannot afford to hire specialized teachers for each particular course, we instead find well-rounded teachers who are talented enough to instruct our students in a multitude of topics. We believe that all of our teachers should be, at a minimum, as well educated as our graduating students, and should therefore be competent enough to teach any subject that our students are being asked to learn. To ensure that this is so, we thoroughly test our teachers prior to hiring them, and all of our teachers are required to fulfill continuing education requirements that are enacted each year by the three administrators.

As for Languages, all of our students learn Latin as well as one additional foreign language of their choice before they graduate. Master Searles pushed Latin for a number of reasons. Fluency in Latin, the source of all other Western languages, will enhance our students' comprehension of the English language and any other foreign languages they choose to study. It will also help our students later in life when they encounter legal, scientific or medical terms that are Latin-based. But lastly, and perhaps most importantly, Master Searles pushed our students to learn Latin because it was hard - or at least perceived to be hard. Learning to speak and write in Latin tends to give our children an earned self-esteem and a feeling of superiority amongst our kids when they compare themselves to the students in other school districts.

Incidentally, it was one of our students, while studying for his Latin class, who came up with the name for our community. He discovered that the Latin word "topia" means "place". After relaying this information to some of his classmates, the group of them began to call our community by the shortened name "The Tope," and somehow this name spread and became accepted by our entire community.

But let's get back to The Academy. Getting the parents actively involved in the educational goals of their children was essential. In addition to an active PTA that meets once every two months we invite all the parents to attend The Academy in a special evening session once each semester. The parents attend classes with each of the teachers of their child for every particular subject, spending a half-hour at a time discussing the coursework and asking questions. Parents are encouraged to become familiar with the coursework that their children are bringing home with them each day and to supplement the efforts of the teacher with at home parental schooling, whenever feasible. This has the dual effect of helping children master their assignments, and of providing the parents with some remedial education. It also serves to place an emphasis on the importance of learning within each household.

Master Searles also decided that we needed a simple dress code. All students are required to wear collar shirts, slacks or skirts and dress shoes. And we do not allow visible undergarments or clothing that is torn into rags - intentionally or not. We do not permit our students to exhibit any piercings, tattoos, or other similar abuses to the human anatomy. All students, male and female alike, are expected to keep themselves well groomed at all times.

Now I know that some will complain that this is too authoritarian, and that we need to allow children to express their individuality, but we believe that there is plenty of time for them to do so after graduation. We are more concerned with teaching our children behaviors that will allow them to succeed in the outside world. And dressing for success is part of that equation. We have also found that when children are forced to dress respectably, they feel more respectable, and have better attitudes within the classroom.

Speaking of behavior, when we set up the Academy, we wanted to put guidelines in place that would dissipate the severe behavioral problems that characterize most public school classrooms in this country. We felt that we had to take control and establish disciplinary procedures from the very start. Master Searles devised several forms of discipline. The two primary punishments are Academic Detention and Disciplinary Detention (AD & DD). AD is given out to a student who has failed to prepare properly for a class on any given day. That student is required to stay after school as long as is needed to finish the neglected assignment and any new homework for the following day. DD is given to students who have behaved improperly, and the punishment for this is usually some sort of manual labor within the Academy. For especially egregious acts, a teacher or administrator can assign a student to Saturday DD, in which that student spends the entire day at the Academy.

In addition, children who cannot control themselves in the classroom are removed and placed in a hyperbaric sound isolation booth located outside the Headmaster's office for the remainder of the class period. These booths, sort of like solitary confinement, have been affectionately nicknamed "the penalty box" by our students. While some may see this as being cruel, we believe it is far crueler to allow an individual child to disrupt an entire classroom and prevent the other children from learning.

Look, our children are not saints. They make mistakes from time to time just like any other children. But the important difference between us and most inner city public school systems is that we act on these mistakes; recognize them, correct them, and attempt to mold future behavior in the proper direction.

One other disciplinary tool that we have at our disposal for many of the students is deviously simple - the telephone. With the advent of the cellular phone, most parents can be instantly contacted if their child misbehaves. The power of proud and caring parents to chastise their own son or daughter at such moments is often greater and far more effective than any punishment that we can administer ourselves. Teachers have come to realize that they merely need to hold up the cell phone, and the implicit threat will more often than not quell a disruptive or unruly student.

Another thing that distinguishes The Academy from most American public schools is that it is not only for children. We encourage all family members, regardless of age, to attend classes as they see fit to further their own education. We have many classes at night and on the weekends specifically geared towards working parents. Most of these classes are taught by Urbanista volunteers and can be anything from basic math or remedial reading to general accounting. There is also a lecture series that is presented in the evenings and is open to all.

Although there is a great deal of emphasis in educating the entire community, most energy is devoted to the school age students. At the end of the year, students and parents are asked to rate the performance of their teacher. These responses, combined with the students' test scores are entered into a database and the results are placed onto the community Web site so that future parents can use this data to make their determination for the next school year. Parents are also encouraged to write any comments about a teacher that would be helpful to future parents. In order to streamline the web sites, only the best and worst of these comments are posted; the CEA gets to select three of the most flattering praises and the opposing CEA is allowed to select three of the most damning criticisms. This procedure is repeated year after year as the child moves from gauge to gauge.

And we achieve a number of positive results through this simple mechanism. First of all, it forces the parents to get involved with the child's education, since up until the sixth gauge, the parents are the ones who make the teacher selection (from sixth to first the student is allowed to decide as part of the effort to teach personal responsibility). Second, it creates a free market atmosphere for the teachers and the CEAs - if the teacher doesn't attract students to his or her class, the CEA knows that something must be done, and if he doesn't, the Headmaster will notice and do something to him. We have no such thing as tenure at The Academy, and we do not tolerate a teachers' union. So we are free to dismiss teachers who are unable to teach, and we generously reward those who can, since pay rate is tied to the success rate of their students.

Since we are a charter school, we have a great deal of leeway in who we can hire for these positions as well. We do not, for instance, require our teachers to be licensed. This allows us to hire recent college graduates who may be brilliant, but who have no teaching degree. Such people often teach at The Academy for a few years, earn enough money to pay for graduate school, and then continue on with their preferred profession.

At the beginning of every school year, Master Searles assembles all of the lower gauge students in the Rectory and delivers an address. Although it changes from year to year, it is always roughly the same. It goes something like this:

> *Good morning students! Tomorrow you will begin a new school year. As you head into your classes I want you to keep one simple truth in the back of your minds. LIFE IS NOT FAIR! If life was fair, we would all be born to wealthy parents and would have anything we wanted or needed handed to us on a silver platter. But it isn't. SO GET OVER IT! I want all of you to know that in the world outside of this school and outside of The Tope, there is corruption, nepotism, racism, and old-boy favoritism that goes on every day.*

> *And it isn't fair to those who are excluded by those practices.*

BUT IT HAPPENS just the same. You can try to fight it. And you should! But you probably won't win. So you'd better have a back-up plan.

As you begin to go out into the world, first when you apply for and attend college and then when you apply for and begin your first job, you will be competing against others who are much better connected than you. The preconceived notions that others have of you will further hinder you, since you come from the inner city and have attended an urban school system. It is not good enough for you to be just as good as all those others. YOU MUST BE BETTER THAN THEM. You must be smarter, more devoted, harder working, and better mannered or you will never stand a chance.

*The good news is that those of you who manage to graduate from The Academy will possess all of the skills you will need to succeed out in the world. It will not be easy to get there. But we **will** get there - together.*

So I've got news for all you parents out there in the suburbs. You'd better get your own schools in order because our kids are coming. And they are well-educated, diligent, well-mannered, un-medicated, and tough as nails. And if your children are not up to snuff, our kids are going to kick their butts!

The Scholars

We wanted to ensure that any of our children who had worked hard to graduate from The Academy were able to attend college, if they were so inclined. All of our children are constantly encouraged to continue on to college, since we feel that a college degree has become almost a necessity in being able to find a high paying white collar job. But we needed a way for these young men and women to be able to pay for tuition, room, board and other expenses. It would do no good to push our children to excel in their course work while attending The Academy if they met the disappointment of not being able to attend college through lack of funds later on.

We also wanted to expose our older school children to the white collar work environment, so that they would be familiar with what was awaiting them after graduation. This would help them to build contacts for either future employment or job references, and it would also let them see first-hand if they liked or had aptitude for a particular type of job, prior to committing to it at college. Once again, we tapped into our corporate sponsors to solve this particular dilemma. The Lucia Foundation was approached, and after numerous meetings and workgroups convened on the issue, a scholarship fund was established to fund college attendance, and a system of internships was devised for our lower gauge students.

This is how it all works:
As soon as students at The Academy reach the sixth gauge in all of their core area subjects, they are allowed to apply for internships with any of our corporate sponsors who have committed to the program. If accepted by a company, the student spends summers and school breaks working for that company. First gauge students

can also spend as many as two days a week during the active school year working for their sponsoring company as well. The student is initially paid minimum wage for the hours he or she works, and is expected to save this income for future use at college, to pay for any incidental expenses. When it comes time to apply for admission to colleges, a student will have a pretty good idea of what profession he or she wants to pursue, having spent a good deal of time in a related internship.

Once accepted to a college, the student then applies to the Foundation for a scholarship. The application form, similar to a college entrance application form, includes the student's school records, test scores, essays, intern history, employee evaluations, etc. Individual sponsors then review these applications and often ask candidates to come in for face to face interviews. Finally, the sponsoring company indicates whether or not it wishes to sponsor a particular individual. On average, students receive between three to five favorable responses. It is then time for the student to make a choice. Once the student selects a sponsor, legal commitment papers are drawn up establishing a contract between the student and the sponsoring company.

The company, for its part, is required to finance the tuition expenses for that student until graduation, as long as a passing grade point average is maintained. The student is obligated to major in a field of study specified by the sponsoring company, and may even be required to enroll in particular courses selected by that company. He or she also commits to three years of employment at that company after graduation. In addition, the student is encouraged to work as an intern at that company during summers and school breaks. Well that covers tuition expenses.

What about room and board? Individual students are encouraged to apply for student assistance from their college, and grants and scholarships from a myriad of other sources. And a number of our parents who have gone through the process with their own children, as well as some of our Urbanistas who have gone through the process themselves have set up a guidance counseling office in The Center to assist interested students in finding and procuring these funds. But this is often not enough.

And so The Foundation approached our community Savings & Loan and requested that they set up a student loan program. Through this program, students are given low interest loans to cover any costs not covered by the corporate sponsors, school financial aid programs, scholarships, grants, and the student's personal savings. The Foundation acts as the co-signer on the loan, and in return, the student is required to enlist as an Urbanista volunteer in The Tope for a three year period immediately following graduation. The loan has a twenty year period for repayment, but a student can reduce the principal, while living in The Tope, by performing any number of community service functions.

Of course, there are instances in which students are either unable or unwilling to stay in our city after graduation - either because they have received a lucrative job offer in another city or because the sponsoring company has requested that they relocate. In the first instance, the sponsoring company and The Foundation must be immediately compensated for their respective investments. Most of the time, this is a big enough disincentive that the student elects to remain with the sponsoring company. In the latter instance, because the student is maintaining the commitment to his or her corporate sponsor, The Foundation waives the Urbanista enlistment requirement and allows the student to relocate.

Now a lot of outsiders will see these programs as a sort of indentured servitude, and in a way it is. But it is also a means to get our kids a college education. And after their three years are up, they are free to live and find employment anywhere they like. We have found however that most students like the structure and like knowing what to expect, and are relieved that a job is awaiting them after graduation. And we will encourage our college graduates to return to The Tope after their commitment has ended. This after all is what we have always wanted.

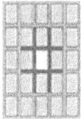

The Urbanistas

I just realized that I have mentioned The Urbanistas several times already, but haven't yet explained who they are. Well, The Urbanistas are a diverse group of people who all have one thing in common: they need an inexpensive place to live here in the City and they are willing to volunteer their time to help defray the cost. Who are they? They are students, single professional mothers or fathers, retired couples and widows, recently unemployed, young people who are just entering the workplace.

Although we prefer to have people who are dedicated to the community, we are not above enlisting Urbanistas purely for their talent alone. We at The Tope are, after all, believers in the free market and realize that it applies to us as well. You get what you pay for. The Urbanista program creates a sort of symbiotic relationship between the enlistee and the community. From the point of view of the enlistee, he or she gets a clean, safe apartment in the middle of the city at a rental price that is well below any other comparable housing in the local market. Urbanistas also build up equity capital in their apartment during the years that they are enlisted in the program. After several tours of duty and the accompanying reenlistment bonuses, an Urbanista can often build up enough savings to be able to put a down payment on a home or pay for graduate school. Only the rent controlled havens of the wealthy compare to this deal.

From our point of view, we bring an intelligent, hard-working individual into the community for three years - the required period of enlistment - who is then given the task of either tutoring students from the Academy, or teaching remedial courses to the

Masters. Can an Urbanista leave the community before his three year term is up? Of course he can. As long as he continues to honor the teaching commitment, he can move out of the community at any time. If however, an individual wants to break the commitment entirely, he will violate the contract and will be required to repay the community for the rent that has been subsidized. This is calculated by figuring the market rate for the apartment rented minus the actual rent paid and multiplied by the number of months. This can become a staggering figure, and is usually a big enough deterrent to prevent this from happening. But by and large this is unnecessary, since our Urbanistas are usually quite content with the arrangement. Not only do they get to live in a secure, vibrant community, they also get the fulfillment that comes with helping to improve the lives of other people through education and opportunity.

In addition to the Urbanista apartments, we have also set aside a fixed percentage of our available housing stock that we sell outright as co-op units to anyone who is willing to pay the price. We felt that it was essential for us to do this so that we could encourage more affluent people to assimilate into our neighborhood over time. However we wanted to deter the process of gentrification that often occurs in rehabilitated urban districts. So we set a minimum threshold of 10% and a maximum ceiling of 20% for the number of these units. We felt that this was a workable ratio that would allow enough talent to come in, but would preclude the lower income people from being squeezed out.

Although the people who buy these units are not required to do so, most of them are coerced by the Block Bouncer to volunteer their service in one way or another. It is a way to integrate these people into the daily life of The Tope. Almost without exception, each of these individuals has knowledge or experience that is valuable to the other less fortunate residents; be it the business savvy of an entrepreneur, the security consciousness and integrity of a police officer, fireman, or military retiree, the wisdom of a university professor, or the life experience of an elderly couple. All of these people have something to offer the community. And in return, the community embraces these people and accepts them into the cultural stew of our small society.

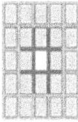

The Hanging Gardens

One of the things that we realized when we started building our first Homesteads was that there was a great deal of wasted space on the rooftops of our buildings. Most of our buildings are brownstone walkups three or four stories in height, and as such typically have a low-sloped roof covering the entire building. After a little research, we found some roofing products, suitable for low sloped roofs, which had walkable and durable surfaces that allowed us to utilize these roofs for a number of useful purposes.

One of our pioneer Urbanistas happened to be a landscape architect and was intensely concerned with environmental issues and beautification via vegetation. She came up with the idea of transforming the roofs into gardens by building up planting beds off of their surface. In some instances it was necessary to re-engineer the roof structure to accommodate the additional load, but this was easily done during the course of restoration. In an urban environment such as ours, the ability to grow flowers, vegetables, and herbs was almost intoxicating to our residents. The practice spread rapidly and now practically every building in our community has some sort of "hanging garden" of one kind or another. On some blocks, where adjoining buildings are roughly the same height, wooden footbridges have been built to connect roof after roof. One gentleman has even created a vineyard complete with a miniature wine making operation.

Our elderly Homesteaders especially enjoy tending to the gardens and also enjoy teaching our children how to grow and tend to the plants, and the importance of keeping the weeds out. And they often use such opportunities to impart some of their wisdom and provide guidance to those who need it The Homesteaders have also set up annual "Best Roof in The Tope" competitions to showcase their gardening expertise.

As a side benefit, these rooftop gardens reduce the amount of stormwater runoff that comes off of our roofs, thereby alleviating the stress on the aging municipal stormwater system. They also reduce the amount of money that our residents need to spend on fruits and vegetables. Many of our residents have learned how to can this produce, and have formed informal trading and bartering groups in our community.

Master Alger, the landscape architect that I mentioned, also requested that we institute a strict recycling program in The Tope. At first there were grumbles, but there were also enough of us who felt that it was important, that we held the day. Every Homestead in The Tope is now equipped with special recycling equipment in the kitchen that crushes metals, pulverizes glass, and shreds and compacts paper into separate compartments. Once a week, the E-man comes and collects all of these packages. He then sells them to various recycling sites around the city, and gives a percentage of his profits back to each resident – thereby encouraging them to recycle more. So not only are we helping to save the environment, we have also created a cottage industry in the process. Synergy at work again!

Well what about all of the other garbage, you ask? We have one other container in the kitchen that also gets picked up by the E-man. All vegetable scraps, waste meat, bones, etc. are placed in a degradable paper bag that is hauled to the autocomposter at The Furnace every two or three days. The autocomposter is a device that was invented by Master Alger and developed with the cooperation of one of our corporate sponsors. In it, all of these bags are chopped up, heated, and mixed with chemicals and biosolids from our waste-water treatment facility. I don't know all the details, but I do know that within several hours this mixture is converted into prime planting soil for the gardens. We have nicknamed this product "Soil-N-Greens" and we plan to start marketing it to the general public, since we now have more of the stuff than we know what to do with

After all of these recycling procedures were in place, we began to receive complaints from the city sanitation department. They wanted to know why we had no garbage to pick up. This department, you see, is dependent upon our wastefulness. They felt that their jobs would be threatened by such efficiency, and they were right. At first they wanted to co-opt the job that our E-men were performing, but we knew that they would only mix our recyclables in with all of their other trash and take it to the landfill. So we went over their heads and argued our case to the Mayor. In the end we won - not because the mayor was overly eco-sensitive, but because the city landfills were nearing capacity and the City was having trouble finding dumping sites for all of its garbage. Having an area of the city that produced no garbage at all suddenly started looking pretty good.

The Infirmary

The first settlers of The Tope became so frustrated with the medical treatment they were getting - or rather **not** getting - at the local clinic, that they asked the Bouncers if it would be possible to set up our own small out-patient clinic, which we now refer to as The Infirmary. They enlisted a couple of interns from the local medical school into the Urbanista Corps and also managed to lure a retired physician, Master Benedict, into the community. Medical supplies, pharmaceuticals, and equipment were donated by a number of our corporate sponsors. In addition, several of the Homesteaders chose to fulfill their community work requirement by becoming assistants to the doctors in this clinic.

While helping the doctors and the patients, they learned valuable nursing skills, and some of these people started to attend night school, and eventually became licensed nurses and EMS technicians. Synergy strikes again!

Over time, Master Benedict was able to hire additional general practitioners at the Infirmary, as our population grew and the demand increased. And once Nightingale House was firmly established, this need grew even more. Initially, most of the assistants' time had to be spent filling out all of the governmental paperwork that is required in order for the doctor to receive Medicaid and Medicare payments. After a while, though, Master Benedict told them not to bother. He felt that the assistants' time was better spent administering to the patients, and so he decided that every patient who came in would be asked to make a minimal cash payment. Those who could, were asked to pay in full. In exchange, Master Benedict required each patient to sign a waiver that prevented them from filing claims against him other than for negligence, and only up to s stipulated maximum. This allowed him to keep his insurance premiums low, and allowed him to charge much lower fees to his patients as a result. And the federal government was cut out of the process altogether. Master Benedict explained that he had to make only enough money to pay his expenses and to pay the interns a meager salary.

In the old days, he told us, before Medicare and Medicaid, before the Feds decided that they needed to regulate everything, most doctors took in elderly and lower income patients exactly the same way. If people could, they paid for the treatment, but if not, the doctors simply looked at it as an overhead expense. And most people were proud enough that they wanted to pay the doctor what they could. You see, most doctors are committed to helping people with their medical problems, above any other concerns - even financial ones. And they will go out of their way to find a way to get care to those who truly need it.

Nowadays though, lower income people have been trained, through years of dependency, to expect any treatment, drug, or test, regardless of the expense, as their absolute right - free of charge or obligation. Worse than that, every drug addict knows the right symptoms that he needs to describe to a hospital physician in order to get a fix; and any parasite looking for a meal, maid service and a nice warm bed, need only to check themselves into the nearest emergency room with a fictitious ailment. The doctors on call don't dare refuse them, for fear of a lawsuit.

And as long as these doctors can fill out the paperwork correctly, the Federal government reimburses them anyway. But God forbid they make a mistake. The federal investigators will immediately go after them for Medicaid fraud. So doctors need teams of trained assistants to help them fill out the forms. But whose wallet do you think the money to pay for all this comes from?

To get back to our Infirmary, though, our doctors and nurses can treat only relatively minor, run of the mill type ailments. They cannot perform major surgery, or advanced testing like MRI's or CAT scans – such patients have to be sent to a larger hospital facility outside of The Tope. But because our Infirmary performs a lot of preventative care examinations; and because we have so many fewer injuries related to gunshots, knifings, beatings, etc.; and so few ailments related to drug and alcohol abuse, as compared to the typical inner city neighborhoods, the rate at which our residents need to be admitted to hospitals is so far below the average as to be laughable.

A large percentage of the people living in The Tope are the so-called "working poor." Their income levels do not qualify them for Medicaid and their employers usually do not provide health insurance. We also had a number of Urbanistas who did not feel it was cost effective to buy into an insurance plan since they were young and healthy. Master Benedict came up with the idea of creating a sort of medical stock market for these people. He contacted some of the doctors that he knew at the hospital, who also became interested in the idea, and they in turn, talked most of the other doctors in the hospital into participating.

Here's how it works. Every person in The Tope who elects to participate in the Medical Savings Market makes a small weekly contribution to the fund. In turn, that individual accrues Medical Units that relate to the cash value of the contribution. The doctors assign values based upon these Medical Units to all of their procedures and treatments, which is based on the current cash value of the MU. And the value of the MU rises in proportion to the average cost of medical services. To account for inflation, the pool of money contributed into the fund is invested in a diverse portfolio of stocks and bonds that is managed by Master Jordan. The doctors love this system because it allows them to treat people without dealing with the insurance / HMO bureaucracy – which can often consume nearly half of all their time and resources. The patients love it because they have a tax-free medical savings fund that has actual cash value, and they themselves, rather than a faceless HMO administrator, are given the power to choose whether or not they need a procedure or treatment.

Since the majority of the people who contribute to the plan are young and generally fairly healthy, the fund has grown nicely in the past couple of years. Although each participant accrues their own account of MU's, ten percent of each contribution goes into an emergency fund that can be used by any participant who suffers a catastrophic illness, the treatment for which exceeds the available balance in that individual's account. And so you see once again, how we have unexpectedly improved one facet of our community structure, by addressing problems in others. And thus we improve the efficiency and operating costs of the entire neighborhood.

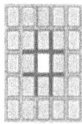

Nightingale House

Perhaps the biggest problem that looms over American society in general and urban communities in particular is what to do about the growing numbers of elderly people and how to care for them in their later years. Social security and Medicare will never cover the medical costs for those who need full-time nursing care. Compounding this problem is the fact that people are living longer and saving less. This is especially frightening when one considers that the numerically immense baby boom generation is creeping nearer and nearer to retirement age.

Our solution to this problem came from an unlikely source - a group of Homesteaders who had fulfilled their community service commitment by working in The Infirmary and assisting our elderly residents with daily chores. These men and women eventually earned degrees and became registered nurses. After one of their parents became ill and needed to be cared for on a full-time basis, one of them thought of the idea of starting a nursing home within The Tope. After this idea was presented to the entire group, they began to research a variety of retirement and nursing care options, before eventually deciding that the "continuing care retirement community" model best suited the conditions that existed at The Tope. Master Jordan at the S & L was approached, and he helped them devise a business plan and to acquire the necessary startup capital that allowed them to establish their company, which they called Nightingale House.

The Continued Care model of nursing care is essentially an insurance policy that guarantees lifelong shelter and health care for those who enroll in the program. Thus catastrophic health care costs are spread out amongst a diverse community of policy holders. In order to make the program economically viable a number of requirements must be met before a contract is granted. Those who wish to buy into the program must do so prior to a specified retirement age. Otherwise, they are required to either pay a lump sum (in the case of our more affluent residents) or pay an additional monthly fee until they begin utilizing the program. This requirement is pro-rated, so that individuals who came to The Tope at an advanced age are not shut out of the program.

In addition to this, the Homesteaders who enroll in this program must secure a reverse mortgage on their co-op apartment which provides funding for the nursing care on an as needed basis. Upon the death of that individual, unless there is a surviving spouse or dependent child, all remaining equity, minus a ten percent profit margin that goes to the S & L, and a twenty percent estate benefit that goes to the heirs, is distributed equally between Nightingale House and the Infirmary. And the Lucia Foundation is given the right of first refusal to buy back the title of the co-op unit at market price.

Homesteaders who elect to enroll in this program operate completely independently from Nightingale House until a health or mental problem triggers the need for some level of care. These individuals know that if they become sick, frail or begin to lose their cognitive abilities through the aging process, their health care needs will be met. By signing up with Nightingale House they enter into an "extensive" contract with the nursing company that covers housing (if and when this becomes necessary), medical services, nursing care, and access to rehabilitation programs.

Upon enrollment in the program, Homesteaders are given a thorough medical exam by one of the doctors in The Infirmary. Exercise and dietary programs are set up to help that resident live a long and healthy life Such a regimen also helps to minimize the number and duration of individuals who will need to make use of the nursing care options, and thus increases the profitability of the company. Those who enroll in the program are also required to undergo yearly follow-up physicals at the Infirmary.

However, when the time comes that an individual cannot function independently without some degree of nursing care, the Assisted Living Phase of the program kicks into gear. People in this phase of care may need help bathing, dressing, cooking meals or doing household chores, but are otherwise fully alert and mentally capable. The Nightingale nurses at this phase provide limited personal care at the Homesteader's residence to help them with their daily activities as needed. These nurses have varying degrees of expertise. Some are novices who are assigned to simply help a resident with a particular chore, while others are licensed nurses who have been trained to give medical attention to the elderly. It all depends on the need of the particular individual receiving the care.

When a Homesteader becomes so sick or mentally incapacitated that full-time nursing care is required, the individual is relocated to Nightingale House, an apartment building located directly adjacent to The Infirmary. Although this relocation is sometimes only temporary, in most cases the move is final. Consequently, many of the individual's belongings are brought into their new room to lend a degree of familiarity and comfort to them.

During this phase, skilled care is prescribed by a physician from the Infirmary and provided by a registered nurse or licensed practical nurse. And all meals are planned and provided by a licensed nutritionist. Nightingale House also has a staff psychologist who assists the Homesteader and his family in coping with the situation, There are also resident therapists who arrange for physical, respiratory, occupational, and speech therapies as needed.

Nightingale House is a real success story for The Tope. Not only is it providing a long-term care option for our elderly residents – approximately 95% of our residents above the age of 55 are currently enrolled, and nearly half of those above the age of forty - it is also an economic engine that is providing jobs for scores of people, both from within and outside our boundaries. It has become so successful, in fact, that the management team has started to take on people who do not actually live within our boundaries; and they are considering setting up a satellite facility elsewhere in the City.

As you can see, a side benefit of this program is that it provides a means for the Lucia Foundation to regain control over and recycle its housing stock and to acquire new properties outside the initial boundaries. In the end, this program is to everyone's advantage.

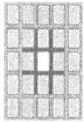

The Watch Tower

The Watch Tower is the nerve center of The Tope. It is the place where all of our security is coordinated and controlled. The actual location of the Watch Tower is a closely guarded secret that only a select group of people is informed about - on a strictly need to know basis. However, every member of the community, from the oldest, most infirm Master, to the youngest child, knows several ways to contact the Tower.

As I have mentioned, The Tope is wired with just about every piece of electronic security device that you can imagine and a few that you could not. All of this equipment is connected back to the Tower, and the Tower, in turn, connects back to all of the Sentry posts, handheld communicators, and to every household through a computer-operated interface. They also have direct lines to the local police station, fire department and rescue squad.

In the Watch Tower, our Guardians can instantly switch on a monitor, when necessary, that will give them a live view of any street in The Tope. In an emergency, they also have the capability of switching on one-way audio to any home or group of homes and can therefore quickly mobilize the community to take action. Individual residents have the capability to manually switch on two-way communication if necessary, and can do so by voice command, if this becomes necessary for any reason. .

All homes and stores in The Tope are also equipped with smoke, heat, and carbon monoxide detectors that are wired to the Tower. In addition, every resident constantly carries a wireless and silent "panic button" that can be triggered if that individual is in imminent danger. As soon as this button is activated, Guardians in The Tower can pinpoint the location of the alert with their GPS equipment, and summon help. The Tower is manned around the clock 365 days a year by a minimum of three Guardians. These Guardians are employees of The Tope rather than volunteers, because we wanted to make sure that we got the most qualified people in these jobs, rather than the most eager. Many of our Guardians are retired and active-duty military servicemen. Others are city police officers or firemen who are looking to moonlight.

Our first line of defense in The Tope is the "Sentry". A Sentry is a Homesteader who is given the task of patrolling the street. Two Sentries are assigned to each street during the nighttime and one Sentry during the day, and they are in direct contact with the Tower through a hand-held wireless communicator. The Tower can also patch them through to Sentries that are patrolling nearby streets if this becomes necessary. Each member of The Tope above voting age is assigned to Sentry duty approximately once every two months - or as required to fill up all of the time slots.

All that a Sentry is required to do is to patrol the streets, to question any suspicious individuals, and to communicate with the Tower if a situation appears to be getting out of hand. At the perimeter blocks of The Tope, the Sentries are posted at the end of the street, at the gateposts into The Tope. Within the interior blocks, Sentries are free to wander anywhere they like as long as they can view the entire street.

All of this may seem a bit extreme to those who live outside The Tope. But we see it as being a bit like living in the Wild Wild West - there are outlaws and savages all around us, intent on raiding us at any opportunity. The Guardians and the Sentries protect us. But they also serve another vital purpose. They fuel the *esprit de corps* of this community, because once someone has performed Sentry duty, he or she will inevitably feel a sense of personal responsibility for maintaining the safety of The Tope.

Lastly, it is a means for the young people in The Tope to feel that they are an integral part of the community. Since every member of voting age is required to perform Sentry duty, this includes teenagers. In other communities, teens join gangs, wear colors and protect their "hood". Usually this also means protecting their area of drug traffic. In The Tope, we have provided a different means for young men and women to assert themselves. When it is their turn, we assign them to Sentry duty in the evening (from 6 o'clock to midnight), and we pair them with a Master; we usually pair young men with older males, and young women with older females. And by giving them the black beret that signifies Sentry, we also give them a sense of purpose and importance and we let them know that The Tope trusts them to protect and serve our community. To date there has not been a single instance in which this trust was betrayed.

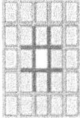

The Wise Men

As you are probably beginning to realize, we have made use of tremendous amounts of high-tech equipment within The Tope. In order to maintain all of this, we needed a fairly sophisticated work crew. And since it would be far too expensive for us to contract out all of these repairs, we decided to do the most sensible thing and train our own people.

We started by enlisting a number of Urbanistas, including a number of our recent college graduates, who had expertise in computers, electronics, industrial machinery, etc. and put them in charge of maintaining equipment that fell within their area of expertise. To assist them in this, we assigned apprentices, who were either students looking to fulfill their vocational training requirements or men and women looking to broaden their marketable skills. And a few of our corporate sponsors also sometimes loaned us their programmers or engineers to help train the entire crew.

This program has now grown to the point where the former apprentices are now teaching new people, and the Urbanistas are used only as advisors, or to teach remedial education courses, intended to bring all interested up to date on the latest technological advances. In a lot of communities or work environments, people with such technical expertise are derided even though they are vital to the operation of normal work and home life. They are called "nerds" or "geeks" and mocked for their assumed lack of social skills. Here in The Tope, we revere people with such knowledge. We decided to call them Wisemen, after one of our residents remarked at a public meeting that it would take a wiser man than himself to fix his broken security system.

But this raises a more important point. In most urban communities young men and women are often castigated and ridiculed for adopting behaviors that would tend to assist them in moving up the social and economic ladder. Conversely, destructive behavior is lauded and admired. Children come to revere the drug dealers more than they do the scholar or the hard-working parent. And they set their sights on becoming professional athletes and gangsta rappers more than they do on becoming a doctor, or lawyer or engineer.

Speaking proper English and behaving politely towards others is considered evidence of "becoming white" while the use of slang and native languages prevails. I once heard Master Searles lecturing a group of ebonically challenged youths who complained about having to learn English grammar and pronunciation. They stated that they wanted to maintain their native African ethnic identity. "African?!?," she yelled at them. "You are not African. You're American. And if you want to succeed in America you'd better learn to speak the language of the successful."

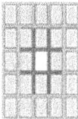

The Center

At the center of the twenty-five square blocks that comprise The Tope, there was an entire block that was almost completely vacant. When we initially prepared the master plan for The Tope we felt that this piece of property presented a unique opportunity to develop into a public park. And so the ground was raked out to remove all debris, some new topsoil was brought in (and mixed with Soil-N-Green from The Furnace), and trees, shrubs and other landscaping were planted. But primarily, this area is a large open lawn where all of the Homesteaders are free to congregate, lounge and play.

We also received permission from the City to close off all through-traffic along the streets that intersected the park. This idea was initially presented to the City Planning Commission as a pedestrian safety issue, but our real intent was to discourage gang drive-by's through the neighborhood - and so far it has worked. At two opposing ends of the central block, The Academy and The Rectory frame the park. On the other ends sit The Furnace, our nickname for our power plant and utility center, and across from this sits our recreation center, which most of our residents refer to as simply The Center.

The Center is a building that houses many different facilities that are vital to the health of our community and our residents. Within it there are basketball courts, a swimming pool, a weight room and workout room, a general recreation room that contains ping pong tables and other donated games, a day care center, shops for woodworking, welding, electronics, automotive repair, ceramics and other crafts. There is also a reading room with an honor system library that houses books and magazines donated by the residents. But most importantly, The Center houses the administrative offices for The Tope, The Lucia Foundation, as well as our main computer network server room.

For a miniscule annual fee, any resident of The Tope can obtain a Rec Card, which provides that individual with access to any facility in The Center. Most of our residents choose to pay the fee, because the benefits of membership are so great. There are activities, workshops, and training classes for just about every interest and for children and adults of all ages. There are also athletic classes for all age groups, and there are athletic competitions that take place here at different times of the year.

The day care center was the brain-child of a group of elderly Homesteaders who in the initial phases of the restoration effort had elected to perform their work commitment by watching the children of parents who were working elsewhere. After their work commitment was fulfilled, these people wanted to continue what they were doing, having enjoyed it immensely. They asked the Lucia Foundation if there was any way that they could set up a permanent day care center as a means to supplement their incomes.

The Foundation thought that this was a wonderful idea - there was an increasing need for day care as more and more parents found full-time employment - and so a space for them was constructed in a large building in the middle of the community that would later become The Center. They still run their day care company out of the same space, paying rent to the Foundation, and receiving a percentage of all revenue taken in through Rec Card fees. They continue to recruit new employees as the number of families within The Tope grows.

In the auto repair wing at The Center, Master Johnson teaches anyone who is interested all about auto repair. Several old clunkers were donated by Foundation members, and these cars have been taken apart and put back together more times than anybody can remember. A number of these cars are rented out to Homesteaders at bargain rates. In addition to the traditional internal combustion vehicles, the center also has two vehicles – a minibus and a mid-sized car that run entirely on hydrogen fuel cells. Master Johnson has been certified as a master technician on these vehicles and he is training a number of young men and women to service these vehicles as well. He believes that these hydrogen cars will become increasingly popular as gasoline prices continue to soar, and he wants his students to be positioned to become the well-paid repairmen for these new vehicles when their day comes.

The aerobics room in The Center is also used to give classes in Defendo, a quasi-martial arts self-defense system that was developed by Master Powell, one of our original Homesteaders. Master Powell came to The Tope after retiring, at age 36, from the Army Rangers. He was elected Block Bouncer, and even served a term as President, and his initial years at The Tope were invaluable for the knowledge that he possessed in defensive techniques. His ability to show us how to secure our boundaries, produce areas of defensible space, and his establishment of Sentry positions and surveillance routes enabled us to get through our formative years with only a few regrettable incidents.

Now, as I said, he teaches his weekly course on self-defense. Although residents are not required to take this course, most choose to do so. In it, Master Powell teaches defensive techniques, such as how to incapacitate an assailant, what actions to take if an attacker has a knife or gun, how to use pepper spray and Tasers, how to fire a rifle and a shotgun, and how to use commonly found objects like keys, pens and sticks as weapons that can incapacitate an attacker. But most important of all, Master Powell teaches people how to avoid a situation in the first place, or if that fails, how to summon help quickly and effectively - utilizing all of the technological gadgets that we residents of The Tope have at our disposal. His students are also taught how to spot potential assailants and what to do to alert The Watchtower and the Sentries.

One of the first things that we did when we established The Tope was to request that the settlers possess no handguns. While we would never dream of forcibly taking away our residents' constitutional right to bear arms, we felt that we could use our bully pulpit to ask them not to own this particular type of weapon. And most of our residents agreed to give up this right in the interest of community safety. This is not to say that we are unarmed, however. In fact, most families here own shotguns or rifles for their self-protection, but they are expected to keep these firearms safely locked away; to be taken out only if the community or an individual is threatened with violence. But handguns, because they are so easily concealed and portable (and thus more likely to lead to rash violence) are taboo here. They are really unnecessary anyway. Since the entire Block reacts to any threat of violence, there is really no need for a small, portable weapon.

Unfortunately, the remainder of the City is not as safe as our twenty five block area. Many of our residents, though agreeing with our handgun policy within The Tope, wanted to be able to carry one when they left the area, for whatever reason. And so we built The Arsenal, a secure building on a perimeter block where handguns are checked in and out by our resident gunsmith, whom we refer to as Master Smith. Master Smith also performs all the maintenance on the guns, makes sure they are properly loaded before they are checked out and unloaded and cleaned when they are checked in, and teaches gun safety classes – a requirement for any Homesteader who wishes to use the facility.

The Arsenal also has a basement firing range where all of our residents are encouraged to practice shooting any of their weapons. And once every year, a marksmanship competition is held in the range. Largely due the influence of Master Powell and Master Smith, The Tope has one of the lowest crime rates of any area in the City. I believe that the word has gotten out on the street that is not wise to commit a crime in our community. Because more than likely, you won't get away with it, and you'll probably get your ass kicked for good measure.

Several weeks ago, for instance, a man from outside The Tope tried to attack a young woman at one of the perimeter blocks. We believe that he intended to rape her, but he never got close to executing his act. Before he knew what hit him, this woman had him on the ground, gasping for air, hog-tied; and within seconds he was surrounded by a large crowd of irate, well-armed, Homesteaders. They wanted to shoot the poor bastard. But the Block Bouncer arrived and calmed everybody down. A police cruiser drove up seconds later and discussed the situation with the Bouncer.

Due to the fact that no real crime had been committed – at least not one that was likely to be prosecuted - and since the situation was under control, the officers decided to drive off to a more crime-ridden area of the city. A decision was made to simply photograph the assailant (so that our Sentries could identify him in the future) and to escort him out of the community. He was warned in the strongest possible terms never to set foot within our boundaries again, and then sent on his way. It was a shame though that the man slipped and fell so many times on his way out!

Now there are some outsiders, who would consider our actions barbaric - they would say that we are acting as judge and jury, and that we should allow the police and the City criminal courts to render a verdict and inflict a punishment for such offenses. Others would say that we are not really solving the problem, just pushing it off to another area of the City. Well we plead guilty on both charges. But you know what, our residents are safe. And because we can defend ourselves and patrol our streets the way we do, our residents have one commodity that other city dwellers do not have - freedom.

Freedom to walk the streets, day or night; freedom to jog in our park without being accosted by a mugger or a rapist; freedom to use an ATM machine without having a vagrant hanging off our arm demanding money; freedom for our children to play outside or walk to school without their parents having to worry that a psychopath or pedophile will abduct them.

These are all freedoms that we Americans once took to be self-evident, but which we have somehow lost one by one. It happened so slowly, but with such regularity that we didn't even notice that it was happening - but over the years, in little salami slices, our freedom was gradually taken away, and soon there was nothing left but the memory.

Well we here at The Tope have taken our freedom back. It wasn't easy, and it wasn't obtained without bloodshed, determination and constant vigilance; but it was worth it. As for the argument that we are not really solving any problems, my response is that we cannot possibly solve such a problem for an entire city, only for ourselves. And if the next neighborhood over wants to band together, and protect themselves as we have, I say more power to them. In fact, there is some evidence to suggest that this is exactly what is happening; another example of the power of synergy. If every neighborhood in the city operated the way we did; if every community supplemented the police force and worked with it, rather than view it as an enemy, there would be far fewer needless deaths, and far fewer children and adults addicted to drugs and alcohol.

Conversely, the police and fire departments have come to realize that they too are safe within The Tope, and react to our residents accordingly. When the fire department is called into our neighborhood, they know that there is little chance that they will have to run into an enflamed, booby-trapped, crack house or methamphetamine lab. And we experience no racial problems with the local police force - our residents are not harassed or accidentally shot at, because the police know that an overwhelming majority of people in our neighborhood are on the right side of the law, their side.

Likewise, our residents, regardless of skin tone, have no problem hailing a cab within the confines of The Tope, since the local cabbies have come to realize that there is no danger of being stiffed, robbed or murdered by our residents. And we have no difficulty getting the pizza man to deliver!

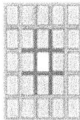

The Rectory

We have one church in The Tope, which we call The Rectory, and it is unlike any other - anywhere else in the world. This is because our church has no priest; or pastor, or rabbi for that matter. Instead, a different member of the community, who is free to select a topic of his or her own choosing, delivers the sermon each week. This person is selected the week prior by our Elder, an elected official, who is in charge of ethics for The Tope.

We call the individual who delivers the address the Beamer, a title that is dedicated to our first Elder, Master Campbell, since departed. Master Campbell liked to say that individual morality is like walking on a balance beam; that each of us knows where to walk to stay on that beam, though it is sometimes difficult, and that sometimes we even fall off of the beam or choose to move off of the beam, since all of us have free will, and are fallible. But most of us know where it is at all times, and how to get back onto the beam if we stumble.

Being selected Beamer for the week is considered a great honor, because in being selected, you have been chosen to embody the moral ideal of the entire community and are deemed worthy of espousing your deepest convictions to all others. And since we have people of all religious faiths in The Tope, we have Beamers who represent all faiths as well. We have found, perhaps surprisingly to some, that different religions are really not all that different in their core beliefs. And that these core beliefs center around ideals of absolute morality that are common to all people who wish to live together in a civic environment. Since a different person is selected each week, the address becomes an event that everyone looks forward to, rather than a bother that one feels obligated to attend. It also keeps the message fresh and dynamic, since the Beamer generally puts a lot of effort into it.

Quite often, the Elder assists the Beamer in writing, editing, and preparing multimedia presentations for the address, for it is important that the message is not clouded by technical glitches or grammatical errors. Most of the Beamers appreciate the Elders input, because they are eager to put on a first rate show. Because for that brief moment, he or she is the center and spiritual leader of the community. It is a responsibility that is understood by all and never taken lightly.

In the addresses that are delivered, the Beamers, in addition to discussing their own religious beliefs, sometimes discuss the foundations of American democracy - the Constitution, the founding fathers, the basis for our judicial system, etc. - and this brings me back to an important distinction, as far as our Rectory is concerned. Our church is fundamentally linked to the legal and political structure in our community, so much so that the individual who runs The Rectory is an elected official. Now I know there are some who would gasp at this notion and begin to spout off about the need for separation between church and state. And I would be the first to agree - if we had a single denomination that wanted to force its own ideology upon those of other faiths. But this is not what we have. All faiths are represented here, including those with no faith, or rather, those whose only faith is the rule of law (and the rules of The Tope).

Most of all we felt that government needed to be tied to our religious practices because one is merely a reflection of the other. One speaks to what we should and should not do, and the other acts on behalf of those beliefs.

The Rectory building itself is quite unusual, since it is a renovated movie palace - one of those Art Deco gems that was built back in the thirties. It is quite ornate, with plaster ceilings, decorative lighting and balconies, but it has been fitted with more modern, and more comfortable theater style seating. We have also decided to leave the concession stand in operation, so that people can buy coffee or tea, and breakfast snacks prior to the address. We see no reason why our parishioners should be uncomfortable while they sit and listen.

The fact that it was a theater provides a number of operational advantages, as well. For instance, many of the Beamers like to use audiovisual aids to complement their address; hooking up a computer to a projector and sound system easily accomplishes this. We also use the space to house any meetings which need to accommodate large groups of people - like our monthly lectures or our annual town meeting and it is also used by our community theater group to present its productions as well as a monthly community movie night.

One of the best addresses I ever heard in The Rectory was delivered by one of the teachers at our Academy, Master Naething. I am paraphrasing this, of course, as it was some time ago. But it went something like this:

> *Let me ask you something. Why do we have laws? I mean what good are they anyway? Why do we need them? Well the answer is that we **DON'T** need them. Or rather, we **WOULDN'T** need them if we lived like every other form of life that exists on this planet. There are no laws in the animal kingdom. Animals kill and steal from each other **ALL THE TIME!** It's a dog eat dog world out there - every beast for himself, family against family, and the quickest and the strongest and the smartest survive. That is the law of the jungle. Survival of the fittest. That is Darwin's law. And though it is brutal, it works.*

> *But we humans are different. We choose to live together in communities and pool our resources and talents. And by doing so, most of us are relieved of the burden of fending for and providing food for ourselves. We are free to pursue other endeavors. And by distributing the collective needs of individuals within the community, we free ourselves to pursue chores that go beyond the mere maintenance of life. We humans*

do not need to spend the better part of our day gathering food for our self and our family because there are farmers and ranchers and food processing plants that supply this food to all of us. While we are out working, we do not need to worry about someone raiding our house and ravaging our spouse or child, because we have military and police forces that protect all of us.

But in order for all of this to work, we need two things - rules of commerce and rules of conduct. Rules that we as citizens all agree to abide by.

The beauty of the American republic is that We the People have the power to constantly adjust both the rules of commerce and the rules of conduct. And we have individual freedom to pursue our own destiny as long as we operate within these rules. "We hold these truths to be self-evident, that all men are created equal, that they are endowed by their Creator with certain unalienable rights, that among these are Life, Liberty, and the pursuit of Happiness." These wonderful words written by Thomas Jefferson have resounded through our country and our people for more than two centuries. And the individual and collective freedom that they have brought about has resulted in a prosperity and morality that is unparalleled in the history of mankind.

We here in The Tope are tasked with the difficult chore of making sure that this prosperity and morality reaches down to everyone - even into the depths of the darkest ghetto. We will find that with prosperity comes freedom. Freedom, however, is worthless if it is not accompanied by morality, because our liberty makes it possible for us to do evil as well as good. Each of us must be vigilant that we as individuals and as a community make choices that are moral, ethical, and just. While our morality is honed individually through our faith and religious beliefs, it is codified collectively through our legal and political systems. And so we all need to respect and support those institutions, and when necessary, demand them to change.

But for us, prosperity and morality should not be enough. They should only be the foundation upon which a far more fulfilling *existence is built upon. We should constantly be searching for beauty and enlightenment, and striving for excellence in everything that we do. This is the essence of Jefferson's pursuit of Happiness made possible by individual liberty. And it is the extra step that will bring us all closer to God.*

There is an old Woody Allen movie in which the main character, depressed and contemplating suicide, decides to list his reasons for living. What he comes up with is the following list:

1. Groucho Marx
2. Willie Mays
3. The Second Movement of the Jupiter Symphony
4. Louis Armstrong's Potato Head Blues
5. Swedish movies
6. Sentimental Education by Flaubert
7. Marlon Brando
8. Frank Sinatra
9. Those incredible apples and pears by Cezanne
10. She Crab Soup at Sam Wo's
11. Tracy's face

Funny. But interesting as well. A comedian, two seminal pieces of music, an athletic marvel, a good book, acclaimed cinematography, accomplished actors and performers, a delicious bowl of food, an art masterpiece, and a beautiful young woman. In a sense, these are exactly the kinds of things that make life worth living. And if everyone in this room sat and thought awhile about what it is that really makes life enjoyable for them, I'd bet that all of your lists would look surprisingly similar to Mr. Allen's. All of these are things that either delight the senses, stir our emotions, or bring us knowledge, and inspire a sense of awe within us. This sense of awe results from the realization that an individual - one of us - has created something of such beauty, stirred an emotion within us so powerful, or performed a feat so incredible that we had previously not been able to imagine it possible.

When we achieve excellence we not only fulfill ourselves, we also inspire the rest of those who look on. And in so doing we come closer and closer to God.

Now go forth and spread beauty and light.

There was more to it of course, for it lasted the better part of an hour. And my recollection doesn't do it justice, as it was punctuated with music and a visual presentation highlighting great works of art, invention, and athletic feats. True to his message, it was at once inspiring and enlightening. I left The Rectory that day with a bounce in my step and a tune in my head and with the determination to excel at the work ahead of me. That is what church should be all about.

Oh, I almost forgot. There is one thing in particular that distinguishes our Rectory from any other church anywhere else in the world. We don't pass the collection plate, or demand a cut of our parishioners' incomes.

Say Hallelujah! Say Amen!

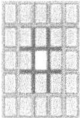

The Furnace

At the center of The Tope, facing the plaza, there is a large building, that we call The Furnace, which houses all of the utility services for our community. This building, a structure composed of massive brick supporting walls and cast iron interior columns, had been an industrial warehouse of some kind at the start of the twentieth century. We have left it mostly intact, and have restored all of the original building features. In doing so, as was the case with the restoration of many of our buildings, we became eligible for Federal and State tax credits earmarked for historic restoration projects. The only change that we made was to decorate the façade with neon lighting and signage, and to add a high tech tower.

Within this building, gray waste-water from individual buildings and homes is processed and then pumped back into our water supply. Telephone, television, and internet services are relayed directly to a high speed internet backbone connection. And electricity is generated with a series of massive hydrogen fuel cell generators. This electricity is supplemented with photovoltaic power generated on many of our rooftops.

For those of you who are unfamiliar with the technology, fuel cells are power generation devices that take hydrogen, usually converted from natural gas, and use it to form an electrochemical reaction - a noise free process. In our case we also use methane gas reclaimed from the solid waste treatment facility located within the same building. The only bi-product of this reaction besides the electric current is water (which we then mix with the recycled water from our water treatment plant) and heat (which is used to provide hot water for the adjacent community-owned buildings). And because the methane gas is converted into hydrogen, and all solid waste is converted into compost, we are not subjected to the awful stench that usually emanates from treatment facilities and power plants. Thus we were able to place it right smack in the center of town.

Fuel cells have been used for a number of years to provide primary power to remote facilities and as emergency power for large factories. One of our corporate sponsors has been developing this technology for years, but has just recently been able to get the unit cost down to a marketable level. They have also developed a smaller scale unit that can be used to propel automobiles and buses. This company decided to use The Tope as a site to perform its field-testing to see if this technology was a viable alternative to electrify a small community, or even possibly an entire city. We were also given a large van that runs on methanol, which we have converted into our community ambulance.

The fuel cells are connected to the electric utility grid serving the entire City. And since we do not use all of the current that is generated by the devices, we sell the remaining current to the local power company. By being on the grid, we also are assured that our community will not lose power if The Furnace goes down. Likewise, if the power grid goes down, an automatic disconnect is switched and power is provided only to ourselves. At such times, since we produce more electricity than we can consume, giant arcs of power are released up the tower, creating quite a show for those lucky enough to see it.

Fuel cell technology will undoubtedly be made available to the greater American public once our field test is complete. My sense though is that it will encounter great resistance. For although many politicians and media personalities constantly blather about the need to save the environment, they are for the most part in the pockets of lobbyists for traditional power companies, "big oil" and OPEC nations. But how anybody could claim to be an environmentalist, while simultaneously permitting nuclear power plants to generate gallon upon gallon of lethal radioactive waste, is beyond me! But somehow they get away with it.

Although fuel cells are a promising new alternate means of producing energy, most people will not be willing to change something so important so drastically, unless they are forced to do so, or unless the financial benefits are overwhelming. So there is sure to be red tape, debilitating regulatory measures, scare tactics and hysteria over the dangers of hydrogen. And I am sure that pictures and video clips from the Hindenburg disaster will be on headlines and our nightly news in an effort to scare people away from it and back to petroleum, coal and nuclear power.

But while the rest of the world will switch to this fuel source only when it becomes an economic necessity, the founders of The Tope were operating under a set of different priorities. First of all, we did not want to be reliant on an outside source for our power, since we did not want a sudden change in energy prices to bankrupt our Homesteaders. Our power generator also had to be relatively small, and most importantly, it had to be clean.

After a lot of research, fuel cell technology was the only logical alternative. But the technology was really still in its infancy, or more accurately, its adolescence. So we contacted one of the major players in the field and offered to help develop and test an urban prototype - ourselves. All electrical power that is generated at The Furnace is conducted to our individual residences via underground cables and transformers, which run in shielded concrete pipes that also carry the fiber optic lines (for telephone, HDTV, and internet service). Placing these cables underground is initially more expensive than running them overhead. But a life cycle cost analysis convinced us to place them underground. Doing so reduces repair costs that would otherwise result from exposure to severe weather, and makes maintenance much easier.

It also eliminates overhead power poles, which are dangerous and unsightly. You would not believe the visual difference that this makes to a community until you see it for yourself.

At The Furnace, as I said, we also incorporated a large tower into the design of the building, as an architectural feature; but this tower also serves as a wireless communication tower, for which we receive a sizable monthly payment from a sponsoring communications company. This goes to show you that with a little bit of thought and consideration you can incorporate new technologies without having them become visual scars on your community. Good design usually doesn't cost much more to build and is so vital to the spirit of the people who inhabit a community. The Furnace is a testament to this principal - so much so that we decided to develop our most public space, The Plaza, directly in front of it. This is because, like most things in The Tope, we are proud of it and want to show it off.

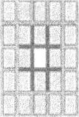

Next

And that, my friends, is The Tope in a nutshell. What constantly amazes me about this place is that it was accomplished without spending a single dollar of taxpayer money. In fact, the community actually turns a profit and contributes more in taxes to the City than it consumes in services. It further amazes me that this community was established and continues to function without any direct involvement from the state or federal government.

It wasn't easy to get this far. But then again, it wasn't really that difficult either. All that was needed was a coherent plan, and a lot of hard work, vigilance, and determination by a group of decent people who banded together to achieve the common good, while pursuing their individual dreams. And the plan itself was pretty easy to put in place. We had no input from any Rhodes scholars or Nobel Prize winning economists - just the collective common sense of the residents themselves.

As I said, we are getting ready to expand. At first this will mean acquiring land concentrically around our current borders. It will also mean that we will have to educate the rest of the urban community as to how we have achieved our success. We believe that The Tope can be replicated just about anywhere, if our guidelines are followed. You see The Tope isn't really a place - it's an idea about what a place should be. And though it is impossible to ever really achieve that ideal in its purest form, a community can transform itself into greatness in striving to become it.

There has been some talk floating around of an effort to start up a similar community in another City. The Foundation has been sending out feelers to some of our settlers, asking them if they would consider relocating. They have asked me as well. I don't know if I have it in me. But I have a feeling that they're going to make me an offer that I can't refuse!

Oh yeah, one more thing! Nancy dropped in to see me the other day and asked me if I was still interested in getting my book published. I had almost forgotten about it, actually. She told me that her company was ready to negotiate a deal with me. She had recently been promoted to Senior Editor at St. Mark's Press, and she immediately petitioned her superiors to publish the book that had started all of this so many years ago.

And that is The News from The Tope! At least for now….

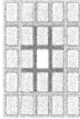

Epilogue

After telling this story, my former classmates had more questions than I could possibly answer in one night. It was getting late, anyway, and our reunion was the next day. Frank had to get back to the hotel room to help his wife with the two kids, while Mike and Alex wanted to travel downtown to the museums and shops. And I was meeting Nancy for dinner at a new restaurant that had opened up back at The Tope. Nancy and I had gotten quite close over the past few years, as we helped to build our mutual dream into a reality.

And so I said goodnight to my friends after inviting them all to visit The Tope the following weekend. I'd gotten the distinct impression that none of them believed my story; that they felt I was perpetuating some bizarre practical joke on them, for whatever reason. But at the same time there was a glimmer of acceptance in their eyes, that the community I had described to them could in fact be a reality. For the process that I had described made imminent and visceral sense to them. They wanted to believe me, but the enormity of what I had described to them was beyond their level of credulity.

In the end, they would just have to come and see the place for themselves

.